* * * *

Someone decides to start a bank of dreams. He thinks what's needed is some way to convert low-voltage goodwill into high-voltage action. He will be a transformer, a currency converter. He will track down small-scale, local-level, non-technical, low-cost community ideas from his imagination and his experience, and from his friends and from around the country, and deposit them into a bank of vignettes, fragments, thought-starters, sparks. Then he'll open for business. Anyone can take out loans or make withdrawals. The idea is to give all his assets away.

* * * *

community dreams

ideas for
enriching
neighborhood
and
community
life

bill berkowitz

Impact 🐚 Publishers
POST OFFICE BOX 1094
SAN LUIS OBISPO, CALIFORNIA 93406

Copyright © 1984
by William R. Berkowitz

Library of Congress Cataloging in Publication Data

Berkowitz, William R., 1939-
    Community dreams.

    Bibliography: p.
    1. Community development--United States--Miscellanea.
2. Neighborhood--United States--Miscellanea. 3. Community organization--Miscellanea. 4. Social change--Miscellanea. 5. Utopias--Miscellanea. I. Title.
HN90.C6B46   1984   307'.3362   83-22853
ISBN 0-905166-29-1 (pbk.)

Cover and chapter introduction art by Diane and Joel Schatz, Transition Graphics, Salem, Oregon.
Additional credits in the "Notes" section, pages 241 - 245.

Printed in the United States of America

Published by **Impact ␨ Publishers**
POST OFFICE BOX 1094
SAN LUIS OBISPO, CALIFORNIA 93406

community dreams

To know the pine, go to the pine;
To know the bamboo, go to the bamboo.

— Bashō

community dreams

skills

Ten in the morning on a side street in town. New building going up. A bricklayer, working with mortar and trowel, putting up a side wall.

A small crowd gathers, a blend of men and women, young and old. The bricklayer turns:

"Now, when you're putting up a wall like this, what you want to do is to make sure that.... You start by.... And when you've got that lined up, then you...."

This is the Tuesday morning bricklaying lesson, brought to you courtesy of your local construction company.

.   .   .

Wednesday, it's welding, Thursday carpentry, Friday electrical wiring. Topics change from time to time; a schedule is posted. If you want to learn a skill, or just watch, all you do is show up. If you want practice, sign up for the apprentice program where you work for free, or sometimes a dollar or two an hour, under supervision. Kids of all ages try this on vacation.

The University of the Sidewalk keeps people on the streets.

.   .   .

At the newspaper office, the Home and Garden Editor sits by the phone.

Today is phone day, and his phone starts ringing before the appointed hour. How do I install tile grouting? Should I prune my fruit tree this time of year? The radiator leaks all over the floor. Why is my paint peeling?

He is Miss Lonelyhearts of the building trade. When the afternoon is over, he has answered 52 specific home repair questions, matched another 19 callers to local suppliers, referred seven callers elsewhere, and promised another five he'd get back to them. That's his homework for tonight.

The sign over his desk says

Save People Money
Create Good Will
Raise Community Competence

* * *

On Saturday mornings, a couple of people gather around a bay of the corner gas station. Once a week, the owner teaches anyone how to tune cars.

About the same time, the local hardware store has clinic hours. Bring in your sick vacuum cleaner, your light fixture, your door latch, your rocking chair, and we'll show you how to fix it, and maybe fix it for you if it can be fixed at all. No appointment necessary. No claim forms to fill out. No charge.

* * *

The clinic idea appears to have caught on. The bakery teaches cake decorating; the antique shop does workshops in appraisal; the camera store holds monthly slide shows; the dentist upstairs will show you how to brush and floss. Somehow, not too many people take advantage of that offer, so several times a year he puts his show on the pavement and fights plaque outdoors.

* * *

In another town, a group of stores combines to hold "demonstration days," with skill-teaching, exhibits, contests, giveaways, diagrams, refreshments, celebrities, discounts.

* * *

Karl Hess: "Material skills have for so long been accepted as merely the purchased property of corporations and the state that seeing them as the ordinary skills of ordinary people in ordinary settings may seem novel or even unsettling."

*　　*　　*

Try Atari carpentry. Sit at home, plug in the module, then learn how to use a power saw or make a simple cabinet. Take a quiz, or (in advanced models) type in a question. The computer makes diagnoses, and it troubleshoots. It has a list of things most likely to go wrong, plus suggested solutions. Explore the world of programmed household skills. If you don't have the equipment, use the set at the local library.

*　　*　　*

Who wants to learn all these skills? Well, you don't have to learn. You can pay for services, just as always. Or you can trade:

I'm calling the skills bank to make a withdrawal. "Hi, I'd like to find someone to put in a new window." The bank gives me numbers to call; I make arrangements. The guy comes over; I can tell he knows about windows, whether or not he's a professional glazier. I watch and ask questions. He figures his time, which comes to 1 ½ units. I sign a receipt, he sends it to the bank, which makes a withdrawal in my name.

I make it up because I'm a tennis coach and people call me for lessons. I sign their receipts and balance my account. Nice how you can get many of the services you need without paying for them. And how you can parlay one skill into receiving a whole bunch of others.

Skills banks, or skills exchanges, are easy, in that the skills are already there, in the community. What it takes is organization, to break down inertia, and to set things up so that people trust each other enough to exchange skills fairly.

*　　*　　*

Two brothers called Click and Clack do a weekly radio call-in show on fixing cars, where they also reminisce about vintage models of old.

The HandiVan travels from corner to corner, town to town, demonstrating skills from the back of the cab.

The local cable station puts on home repair illustrated. Videotapes stay in the public access room. Some of their stuff also goes out as features over the late evening news.

*   *   *

The newspaper teaches skills in series. Special sets of columns march broadly through a general topic, say landscaping. They have dotted borders plus scissors logos, so as to encourage their being kept. When clipped properly, they fit nicely into a binder, tucked into the Sunday edition. The diligent reader, following previews and reruns, can thus accumulate manuals.

The same Home and Garden Editor runs a series on home repair. His colleagues teach finance and job opportunities, electronics and tailoring — and Shakespeare, by newspaper, for credit, one play a week.

The newspaper is packed with instructions and homework. Some say it's starting to look like Sunrise Semester in print. Others say for a local paper, that's the way it's supposed to be.

*   *   *

Schools teach technical skills, even the private ones. All schools practice the laying on of hands. Technical education has educational parity; for if appropriate technology is our end, appropriate technical instruction must be our means.

*   *   *

The local high school gives Domestic Aptitude Tests to its freshman class. The DAT's are a two-day battery of competency tests, ranging from repairing small engines, to building a bookshelf, to caring for small children, to planning a sample week's menu. Performances are observed and graded. Scores go on the record and are printed out for the student with a diagnostic summary, noting strengths and areas for improvement. Student, parents, and guidance counselor meet to discuss results and make domestic plans from there.

Adults come in and take these tests too, as part of the service.

*   *   *

The local vocational school carries a full line of adult course offerings, well-promoted and in demand. The chem labs are open to the public at night. Also, you want some auto-body work? Students will do it cheap. They learn, you get low-priced service. And if you are a nonprofit organization, you can get work done for free. Printing, for example, or upholstering, or machine tool design.

* * *

In summers, kids work. Schools, camps, and employers form cooperative ventures. Some kids take summer apprenticeships in a local trade. Some become suburban VISTA volunteers. Others go to camp to enjoy themselves, learn things too, do small-scale projects. There's computer camp of course, also gardening camp, geology camp, systems analysis camp. All of this goes in the résumé.

Another group of kids, early teens mostly, wanted their own space to hang out. (Nowhere to go in town.) They took a construction course after school, and went together to builder's camp for a month one summer. On their return, they built their own youth center, by themselves, under direction, board by board.

* * *

At the experimental institutes, new household technologies are developed, tested, refined, and applied. Internships there are prized.

* * *

A network of university professors brings hard science to neighborhood groups. The professors, screened for jargon, turn recent research into popular mechanics. Would you like photovoltaic shingles on your roof? Do you want to turn garbage into compost? We'll show you how.

Sometimes a professor goes to a neighborhood home. A group is waiting there, as it would for the Avon lady. Constituents are reached, information is exchanged, action is planned, and personal ties are tightened.

* * *

The pipe bursts at 3:00 a.m. The awakened homeowner calls, and someone appears within the hour. A clever entrepreneur has organized a small squad of moonlighters into a 24-hour repair service. They carry beepers, for they are house doctors on call. If it can't wait till morning, and sometimes it can't, you can get it done now.

It will cost you. That is, unless you have taken out home repair insurance, a form of black thumb protection. You pay a set policy fee, according to the covered items. There are merit ratings, and high risk pools.

*   *   *

County people get together and decide to hire a county handyman to teach skills to anyone who wants to learn. The handyman teaches, but does not repair. He will travel anywhere in the territory and consult on any subject within his job description. He is a county agent, like his agricultural cousin, with different tools.

In the neighborhoods, semi-pro tinkerers tour the streets.

*   *   *

Who has the time to learn all these skills? Well, you don't have to take in everything all at once. Threescore and ten is a long while. You can learn what you want now, and the rest will wait for later.

Is our goal to create Universal men and women? Sure it is: why not? Competence makes people happy. And it ups the chances. When times are tougher, self-sufficiency becomes more adaptive.

*   *   *

The machinist is going for her fifth level certification. She's a master already, but masters need new challenges. Five more grades after this one to the current pinnacle.

You can scout around for a black-belt electrician. Would you choose any less than a fourth-degree surgeon? Does this provide better service to the public? Is this the meritocracy we've always dreamed about?

*   *   *   *   *

neighborhoods

The newsletter under my door tells me what's going on in my neighborhood. It has short news notes and a calendar of events (special preview of upcoming yard sale; party for Blossom Street residents this Saturday night). There are editorials, rebuttals to the editorials, letters of thanks, letters of outrage. John is moving Monday, could use assistance. Please keep your dog off my lawn. A free classified, a lost and found, things to give away, the neighborhood association minutes and agenda. Favorite recipes and fix-it tips, a few one-liners, an occasional cartoon. Real estate transactions. Police logs. New business ideas. Birthdays and anniversaries, anonymous suggestions, the old-timer's corner. Who's New (baby and adult divisions), plus a scattering of out-and-out gossip and innuendo.

It's mimeographed, and it's only four pages every two weeks. Though it's artistically ragged, and grammatically impure, there's nothing I look forward to reading as much. It makes me feel I belong here.

* * *

Would people pay an average of $10 a year (sliding scale) for 24 yearly issues? After a free issue and trial run, yes, they would. Questions now: Should the newsletter take ads? Should it expand to eight pages? Sixteen? How big can it get without losing the neighborhood feel and intimacy that made it a success in the first place?

* * *

When I first started looking for a place, the real estate people gave me a neighborhood brochure, which told me who lived here, what went on, some neighborhood advantages. A promotional piece, but straightforward, not puffed up. I felt drawn in.

The brochure came with a pocket-size directory of services and resources, places and people to contact. And the real estate people, who are linked with the neighborhood association, will take you on neighborhood tours. They'll also give you copies of the neighborhood newsletter, plus the names of some folks with varying points of view, signed up on a list, and ready to talk.

＊　　　＊　　　＊

One agency, needing new business, put together a slide-tape show to entice new residents and entertain older ones. Original music by a local songwriter, sometimes whistled in the streets.

＊　　　＊　　　＊

I first knew my neighborhood was special when I rented my house. The historical society came by with the house's genealogy, the list of people who had lived there before me, done up like a family tree. Common practice around here, even for people who rent. A labor of love for sure, and done very gradually, but once the tree is done it's done pretty much forever. As I became rooted in the past, I felt more responsible for the present. Thank you to the older people around here, for all your work.

＊　　　＊　　　＊

So much love went into the House Tree Project that it had offspring. One subgroup set to work on a neighborhood historical map. The map marks the little-known high and low spots of the neighborhood's checkered past, and pictures some of the older architecture that might otherwise go unnoticed. A sale item. Some other neighborhoods I found out about later put out walking maps and bicycle maps and jogging maps and things-to-do maps, many with photos and commentary.

＊　　　＊　　　＊

Another group started NOAH, the Neighborhood Oral Archival History, an effort to talk to some of the real old-timers while they're still here, to get down on tape some memories and stories going back to the 19th century before they vanish forever. Most of the tapes are now catalogued at the branch library — students often use them on school projects. Meanwhile, some of the older folks come down and speak with school classes or at the kids' story hours.

* * *

The Welcome Wagon rumbles down the block. Well, actually it's a pickup with a canvas top. But unless the recipients prefer an unmarked wagon, it stops for a full-length courtesy call on each new household moving in.

* * *

The neighborhood assembly is the hub of what goes on around here. I'm a member, just like everyone else. The assembly meets weekly, to raise and act on any issue of neighborhood concern.

Anyone can come, anyone can talk, and anyone who's been at two of the last three meetings can vote. In practice, people tend to appear when they have something in particular to say or bring up. There's also an elected group of nine members who are obliged to be there, who generally want and take on more responsibility, but who don't have any more voting power. It's a hybrid system, but it works out well.

Last week's meeting, for example, featured discussions of unleashed dogs and off-street parking, the report from the tree-planting committee, a possible education grant application, and proposals to relocate the neighborhood machine shop and to expand the cooperative grocery store. The big kids were cautioned not to crowd the little kids' playground space. A few referrals to the community mediation panel were made, and a couple of new informal task groups started. Next week will be the semi-annual municipal performance review; more people will be there then.

* * *

No two neighborhood associations are quite alike. Some have set up 24-hour emergency volunteer services, visitation programs for the sick and infirm, and goods exchanges with neighborhoods nearby. Others run neighborhood study groups, sponsor job-matching programs, and deliver the inter-office mail. A few concentrate more on cultural affairs, give out block awards, and make small grants from their dues.

Most associations belong to the city-wide confederation of neighborhoods which meets once a month to discuss common issues and share new ideas. The associations are also flanked by a network of smaller and more social block groups.

Of course, much of what happens in the neighborhood is informally generated and doesn't involve these organizations at all. But our experience is that the added-on formal structures stimulate more informal ones, which can then get formalized, if there's the need. Formal and informal feed each other, and both serve the common good.

* * *

My neighborhood association is powerful not only because it represents the neighborhood, but also because it gets money from the city council to provide services. Neighborhoods are registered governmental units, with charters, by-laws, the whole works. The combined associations account perhaps for half the town budget. With that money, they are responsible for their own parks and park maintenance, for trash collection, for their branch library, for their recreation and school programs in part, and for whatever extras they want. It's their job to rank priorities, fix budgets, and spend money wisely. Most of the spending is usually done via a contract system, with competitive bidding. The association sets the standards, drafts the contract, hires the vendor, monitors the performance, pays the bills, and decides whether or not to renew.

But there's more than one pathway to neighborhood power. Where I used to live, neighborhoods got vouchers instead of cash, a sort of scrip they could use each year for purchasing services. Then they got bonuses based on how well they did at meeting goals agreed on with the town. (Bonuses went to neighborhood projects.) Also, the association in the next neighborhood over levies a voluntary, graduated tax for small neighborhood programs, over and above the money it gets from the city council. My friend's association goes one step further by directing its voluntary tax dollars to local charities.

* * *

Like most others, my association gets assistance from the town or from local businesses when we want it. We're not timid about asking. Sometimes we also call on our neighborhood "buddy," a neighborhood in another town that's more technically or organizationally advanced. (They've asked us for help, too.)

Beyond this, we've devised inservice training programs for ourselves; for instance, social agencies have come in and trained us in leadership techniques, so that now we're more focused at meetings, with more participation, and things run more smoothly. Then we decided to hold conferences and workshops on special topics like neighborhood enterprise and counseling skills, where we've invited outsiders in and made a few bucks in the process.

*   *   *

Now, industrial recruitment we leave to the Chamber, the big boys. But a group of us has taken responsibility for recruiting small businesses. We keep our eyes and ears open, and when we see a need for another hardware store, or an electronics shop, or a new pharmacy, we'll set to work on finding one, maybe using the multi-media promotional package we designed for those occasions, sometimes even encouraging our neighbors to go into business for themselves.

If it's a question of something which may alter the landscape, even a little, or even if you're not sure, you do have to file a neighborhood impact statement, which has to pass through our neighborhood zoning group. Yet if there's really a need to change the zoning pattern for a desired business — or to protect our residential property — we can usually get it done.

*   *   *

I haven't really talked much about our neighborhood's spirit. We have neighborhood colors, and welcoming signs. People here will adopt-a-house — say some older person's home that needs fixing up — form a work party on a weekend, then fix it up together and christen it with beer. Or they'll rig up an outdoor display — a diorama, or mural, or photomontage of the neighborhood's past, present, and future. Or they'll make an event of handing out the neighborhood fitness awards. Or they'll hold Open House Day, where by tradition all doors are literally open, and anyone can and often does visit anyone else. We believe in rituals like this for warming the heart, and for cultivation of kindliness and grace.

* * *

Most anything that's worth anything gets out to the neighborhood sooner or later. All you need to do is put wheels under it. Start with the artsmobile, bookmobile, jazzmobile, and zoomobile. Shift into the craftsmobile, dancemobile, plantmobile, and jobmobile. Folks turn out for the tennismobile, votemobile, sciencemobile, and carmobile (auto repair). The mobile telescope takes them to the moon and stars....

* * *

The photographer is coming around this week to take pictures for the neighborhood yearbook. Let's be appropriately serious here. Soon you'll be able to see what that couple down the street really looks like, and if so and so is getting older. The yearbook is a big seller. It helps people get to know each other, just like the freshman register at college. The pictures strengthen the neighborhood by giving people faces. Faces lead to greeting. Greeting leads to meeting. Ice is broken; connections are formed.

* * *

The upshot of all this activity is that my neighborhood is more self-sufficient — for we produce more of our own goods; we provide more of our own services; we know what our resources are and where to find them; we've developed talents we didn't have before; and we're less dependent on outside forces, on the turmoil of the outside world. Within pretty broad limits, we can take care of ourselves. And as a consequence, we're better able to take care of others if we need to.

But what is more, my neighborhood is a place where I feel grounded and secure. I'm known, I'm recognized, and I'm accepted. My neighborhood cloaks me, comforts me, keeps me snug on the inside. Someday I may choose to cast it off and leave it behind, or put it in storage, or give it to someone else. Maybe I will. But as long as I take good care of it, it should last me forever.

* * * * *

centers

The community center is on a side street of a neighborhood shopping area, on the first floor of a former beauty salon. It's big enough, though not huge — maybe the size of the grade school gym. Attractive windows, eye-catching signs. Inside, a front desk: "May I help you?" On the right, comfortable sofas and chairs arranged in semicircles. On the left, a long bulletin board, with various notices and events of the day. A coffeepot, always on the house. A corner skylight. Down the aisle, natural partitions set off by furniture, floor plants, and lamps. In back, the administrative offices, a duplicating room, a storage space, another one or two rooms for staff or community group meetings.

Anybody can come in and talk or read or sit. Each is encouraged. In cold weather, a fire is going, and hot cider is on the stove. The quiet games, the constant discussions, newspapers and magazines beckon gently. Some of the bigger centers have recreational facilities in another building or in back or on another floor.

The community center is an indoor oasis, an urban grange. Diversity is its trademark. The first-time mothers group meets in the morning, their kids tagging along — plenty of nursing, bawling, and crawling about. The weight watchers meet in the back room, followed by the anti-nuclear committee, neither of which has offices of its own.

Senior citizens' bingo in the afternoon. Some come early, bring lunch, look over the papers. The public health nurse is there too, checking blood pressures in the same room where the weight watchers met two hours ago. Later on, the merchants association will get together, passing by the gin game out front. Throughout the day, people meet each other by choice and by chance, exchange economic and social rewards, hard assets and simpler lines of credit.

Evening — mostly teenagers now. Rock music twice a week. A small party on Sunday night. Teen sounds, though soundproofed, seep in through where the separated-and-divorced group is meeting.

The landlord is a neighborhood businessperson who rents at half the going rate. The staffing is pure volunteer, what there is of it, since only one person at a time is needed to handle questions and arrange schedules. Most of the furniture and start-up supplies was community-donated. Most operating money comes from fund-raisers, from space rentals to community groups who can afford it, and from contributions — a suggested few bucks a year, more if you can. It doesn't take very much to keep things going.

Most of what goes on is unforced, unpressured, low key. Just a nice place to be, to make yourself at home, and maybe to take part in (or help plan) an event once in a while. Few obligations, but many opportunities. That's why the center succeeds.

* * *

When the traffic got too heavy to bear, the center's directors extended the hours. And they went to time-sharing, more formal than before. In general, mornings for parents and children, afternoons for seniors, evenings for teens, meeting rooms available by appointment. The center was convertible, three centers in one, stagehands changing the set three times a day.

Mitosis was another solution: similar centers in most of the neighborhoods, often smaller in scale. A brisk trade in the import and export of ideas. There are variations, few of them fancy: one center is happy with bar shuffleboard and bumper pool; another shows silent movies and won a soft liquor license. One has a built-in kitchen, and one puts on cabaret.

* * *

Local derelicts come in to the center, carry on or pass out on the couches. The directors decide to build a separate entrance, rent out the second floor, and use it as a shelter for the homeless. People who need a bed rather than the company of others, or who need to dry out, are served upstairs.

* * *

The human service agencies in town have begun to book the meeting rooms more frequently. Why? Because many of their clients like to be seen at neutral locations. Because many don't want to travel, or can't travel, to a central facility, but don't want anyone coming around their home either. Because at the center services are less formal, more human, with fewer role games. Because the people in the community get to know more about the agency. Because the people in the agency get to know more about the community. Because it's often cheaper to give services there — more people can be seen in less time, since you don't have to make appointments by the hour. Because helping behavior is contagious and spreads beyond the meeting room. Some senior agency staff don't especially like the idea of drumming up new business, but others say whom are we working for? They also cite the General Principle: In giving service, mix the options.

So a schedule is posted:

WEDNESDAY
1:00-2:00   Public Health
2:00-3:00   Veterans Services
3:00-4:00   Legal Aid
4:00-5:00   Employment Office

The center staff helps coordinate appointments, evenings and most weekends included. Agencies rotate right through. Most of the time, when they can, they pay a modest rental to keep operations going. And at different centers across town, the same agencies operate with different office hours. Staff move about, like itinerant preachers.

* * *

"This place looks like a multi-service center now," the visitor said, "just like in the human service journals."

"That's how we planned it," the staff person replied.

* * *

Some of the centers, at least the main one in town, are open 24 hours a day, and after midnight serve as sort of a combination late-night diner and hometown traveler's aid society. Neon lights flash after dark. Not too much is going on at two in the morning, but that's okay. A good time to catch up on paperwork, clear the bulletin board, edit the newsletter. A few people do wander in. Occasionally someone will come to crash at the shelter upstairs, or will arrive in real trouble, and the staffer on duty will help or refer.

* * *

In the town hall and also in the library there's a list of spaces available for meetings and other get-togethers. In churches, for example. In basements of apartment buildings, if necessary. In the shopping centers, in office complexes, in the school auditoriums, in some private homes. There's descriptive material and general information on use. If you are looking for a place to meet, find yourself some possibilities, then contact the booking coordinator, who keeps the master schedule, and who will let you know what's free for a given time.

* * *

Smart youth organizer sees no place for kids to go, leases video games and places them in plain view. Ions in the cathode rays lure teen-agers from miles around. Video quarters pay the rent.

The townspeople see a hangout, think of protest. The organizer puts in topical games, like Mideast Invasion and Arms Control. And he installs the Algebra II game, the English Grammar game, the Test-Your-IQ game, the Basic Chemistry game, the Trivia Quiz game, the College Boards game. Teachers give out game assignments.

After a while, even the Live-Out-Your-Fantasy game gets boring. The customers, being more complex than the games, are less boring. They retreat to the back for fast food and talk. And so the youth center was born.

They first thought that the organizer was a really clever fellow. But they were convinced he was unfastened when he turned the center over to the kids, the actual direction and assets. Wrong again. A few adults hang around now as advisors, for legal purposes, and occasional competition.

* * *

At the stroke of 9:30, the record store changes into a coffeehouse. The record bins wheel back to the corner. Folding tables and checkerboard cloths spread out. The espresso machine starts steaming as the house lights dim. New customers arrive. Tonight's blues group begins to warm up. They'll autograph records, and dedicate this one to you.

* * *

The laundromat owner bought some of those lo-noise models so that people using the machines could hear themselves talk. (The dryer vents heat her theater upstairs.) She put biodegradable furniture around the middle so that people wouldn't have to sit in straight lines. Add some original lithographs, backgammon sets, guest appearances, and a stereo in the background, and you begin to restructure the setting.

Sometimes to get people out and together, you've got to cross genetic lines. That's why the laundromat has become a social center. The racquetball club has a juke box downstairs. The supermarket cafeteria serves hot meals family style. The local movie house has a bookshop off the lobby. The bookshop shows movies. The church has card games. The basketball court is a Sunday flea market. The pond in winter is a white dance floor.

* * *

The new owners of the local bar turned up the lighting one notch so that people could see each other just a bit better, put in more back tables, added imports to the repertory, expanded the beer menu, tossed in a set of darts. So people stay longer, drink a little more, spend a little more, talk a little more. If you have the trappings of an English pub, the owners thought, people will come to behave as though they are in one.

* * *

The Neighborhood Tub opened up last month. A communal bathhouse, deliciously warm and steamy inside. Something in the biochemistry dissolves tensions at 102 degrees. Perhaps it's Theory Z, Japan has something. The local Y is wondering about raising its pool temperature a few afternoons a week.

*   *   *   *   *

food

"General! An aerial photograph of the city reveals that many of the buildings appear camouflaged, covered with dense green foliage."
"No, lieutenant, those are rooftop gardens."

*   •   •

Lunchtime at City Hall. Employees head for the roof. Some sit and talk, others strip and sunbathe, others cultivate their gardens. The gardens grow in what used to be children's sandboxes, now hauled skyward. Other parts bloom in rain barrels, hollowed-out oil drums, beaten-up wastebaskets, planters of all sizes and shapes. Vegetables grow on half the roof's surface, and keep the workers below in produce through the summer.

Some sections of the roof garden grow vertically, or hydroponically, without soil. Others employ French culture. They are space-intensive, lovely to look at, the art of the state.

•   •   •

The goal is a self-sufficient and free society. The government believes — the people believe — that you cannot have either one without placing the means of production in the hands of the people.

The people realize that no one is going to place it there for them. So they do it themselves. They start with food. City Hall takes the lead. Rooftops across town follow suit.

*   *   *

From afar, parts of the neighborhood look like a war zone, a dead city now overgrown. But these are gardens again, planted directly in streets that neighborhood residents decided they no longer had use for. So they tore them up, reducing traffic noise and pollution in the process. Many neighborhood streets remaining have garden strips down their newly-installed medians. A subcommittee of the neighborhood association coordinates the planting and works out the labor and distribution systems.

*   *   *

The foods class in the high school has halted production of upside-down biscuits and has gone to forage for edible plants which grow naturally in the parks and on vacant lots and on the outskirts and in the town forest. Today the class eats out. The foods teacher, an ex-botany major, is the outward bound director. The students learn baking, survival, and love of the land.

*   *   *

Most people with any land at all work it intensively, using window boxes, fire escapes, seed flats, grow lights. Those without any outdoor space get first preference for the community garden, a donated stretch of land across from the school. Anyone can sign up for a plot there, a minimum 10' x 15', and maybe larger depending on demand. Your basic $10 fee allows you to farm it for a year. You supply seeds and labor. Tools and fertilizer come included, as does advice from the garden supervisors, a retired couple out there most of the day working their own plot, planting flowers on the borders, and doing a little extra weeding.

*   *   *

Sometimes people grow squatter's gardens in vacant lots, too fruitful to evict.

*   *   *

In basements and guest rooms and unused garages, rainbow trout in tanks glide innocently by. They will soon be eaten.

* * *

The cooperative farm lies on the edge of town. Originally, the co-op members put up a few dollars each to rent the land and buy some hens to lay some eggs. Some eggs became chickens; thus began poultry breeding. Now there are goats and sheep, turkeys and pigs, a slaughterhouse and a smokehouse where members cure their own. The farm takes care of most members' needs for meat. School children learn livestock management. Preschool kids come out to play.

Posted: "This is the town preserve. Be careful! Hunting is allowed in order to foster independence, but only in accordance with the rules and regulations listed below...."

* * *

Grey Bears on the fields at twilight. They are senior citizens, picking up the second harvest, what the first harvesters didn't get. If you have to choose, better people than birds. The produce, good stuff only, goes down to the Golden Age center, where it's the heart of tomorrow's hot lunch. Or it goes to the local soup kitchen, where it feeds the hungry coming in off the street.

In the cities, Grey Bears foraging through the wholesale markets, scouting the exits of food processing companies, prowling around restaurant kitchens. They know the managers by name. They use back doors and pick up what can't sell or won't. They'll take a cantaloupe with a bruise, and take their chances with the peanuts spilled on the floor.

The hungrier bears hit the supermarket trash, neatly laid out by food group, as mutually agreed upon.

* * *

As a child, I was asked by my teachers to bring food for hungry people overseas. Now we ask our children to help hungry people at home. The food collected goes to a local food bank, a storehouse, from where it's sent to senior centers, to parents of babies, to schools for breakfasts, to the soup kitchens, and to homes in need. Some children give up sweets. This is their ongoing hunger project.

* * *

The food bank gets night deposits from hotel chefs and restaurant owners, from bakeries, from air freight companies and health food stores, from local farmers, from cafeteria managers, from fast food chains. Occasionally, the Grey Bears leave something by.

If you don't want to make a deposit, there's a window for negotiating straight-up swaps. A case of green beans for a dozen loaves of French bread. Five gallons of orange juice for five pounds of pastrami futures. The bank deals in most kinds of food currency. And it will trade with other banks in the region for what it needs.

*   *   *

The institutional chefs are in daily contact. When one has extras, the other knows. The school cafeteria sends oat bags to the nursing home. The hospital has leftover egg salad the mental health center can use. Once again, the company kitchen ships fried chicken to the college dorm. Food gets passed around — they used to barter it and keep records, but stopped when they realized that things came out more or less even at the end. They're looking for a volunteer food broker, though.

*   *   *

The vending machines in the corridor are out of Doritos. They have milk, raisins, nuts, fruit, all unacquired tastes. The students protest, claiming their right to choose. The school dietician, backed by administration, says they can choose to go across the street after school. The pro-Dorito faction is in touch with the ACLU.

*   *   *

Parent volunteers serve hot breakfasts at school for kids who choose it, and sit down with the kids and eat it to get the day off to a great start.

In the school cafeteria, some tables vote to have a moment of silence before the meal.

*   *   *

Farmer Brown brings his produce to town (sets up shop in the square on Saturday). Food fresh from farm to you. Another group of more entrepreneurial farmers drives food-laden pickups through the neighborhoods during the week.

When no farmers live nearby, merchants simply buy up leftover goods at the local produce terminal on Friday afternoon, and, passing for old-time ethnics, sell them the next day from pushcarts in the streets.

* * *

The food cooperative started as a modest buying club: members would pre-order their food, drive down to the produce market, load it in a van, truck it to someone's house, sort it out, pick it up, and pay on receipt. As members grew, the co-op rented a storefront; membership grew some more. After a time, the storefront co-op got together with other co-ops to form a federation. They leased a warehouse, where they now buy foods in still larger quantities at better prices, sometimes farmer-direct. The co-ops are big-time food distributors now, but nonprofit, member-owned and operated. Their stores are large enough for the average shopper, but small enough to keep in personal touch with members' needs.

* * *

Inside the storefront food co-op: a children's play space, a combination lounge and meeting area, magazines and coffee, free food delivery to seniors, a trading corner for books/records/clothing, cross-country ski weekends, nutrition exhibits, posted price comparisons, a newsletter at the register, coed softball, folk dancing, a feedback book, and live music on weekends.

* * *

As funds get cut back, the county extension service puts more energy into organizing, networking, and consulting. It helps start a county-wide gardeners' co-op, the yearly fee including a soil test, an on-site consultation, and free admission to the 4-H fair.

Meanwhile, the state agricultural school looks to increase tourist traffic. The demonstration farm on campus highlights the latest in small-scale agricultural technology. Heavy equipment runs on hydro. Light stuff runs on wheat straw. Fish feed off garden sludge.

Community skill levels grow; public sector staff do less direct service and more consulting still.

*   *   *

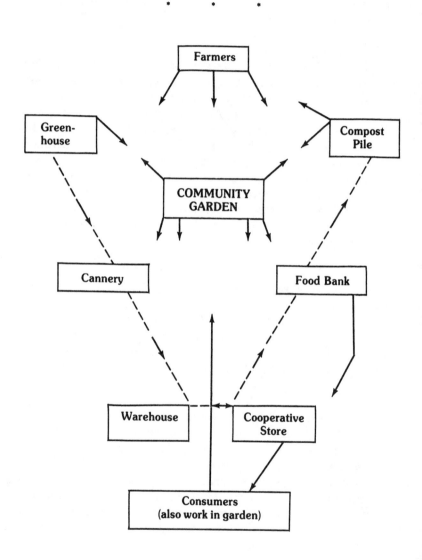

The community garden surrounds the solar greenhouse.

Next to garden and greenhouse is the community canning factory.

Much of the produce, fresh or canned, goes to the warehouse.

The warehouse ships to the cooperative stores.

Bruised goods and surplus are for the food bank.

Inedible residue is for the compost pile. (Some is trucked back to farms for animal feed.)

The compost returns to the gardens.

The town has created a food chain, its own ecosystem.

*   *   *

The bakery is a branch of the food bank. (Too much flour to hold.) Bakers are just bankers minus one.

At night they bake, singing

> *Milk in the batter*
> *Milk in the batter*
> *We bake cake, and nothing's the matter.*

Food bank bakers finishing up their work in the night kitchen take trays of tarts to backed-up early-morning motorists. "Here, it's raspberry, take a bite of this."

*   *   *   *   *

exchanges

When it became clear that much of the problem with goods and services in the community was not with their availability but rather with their distribution, that was when the exchange concept took a great leap forward. It was a matter of setting up the right institutions....

   * * *

Walking down Exchange Place, you pass by bins full of office supplies, cleaning products, garden equipment, baseball cards, video game cartridges, posters, records, power tools, building remnants, plumbing fixtures, paperback books, hardcovers, magazines, bicycles, bicycle parts, skates by size, skiing gloves, football pads, sawdust, pewterware, Tupperware, Hummel figures, carnival glass, old bottles, postcards, lamps, stamps, coins, cassettes, canned tomatoes, toys, comic books, games, puzzles, clothing, cooking utensils, cosmetics, and no-account scrap.

Exchange Place is a thrift shop supermarket, opened just this year. A large rented storefront, counters and aisles. The difference is no cash registers. You bring in an item, an appraiser assigns a dollar value, take it or leave it. Takers get scrip, good for anything in the store. The appraiser, all people who work there, are community volunteers. Since no money changes hands, there's less incentive for partiality. Let's call this Model A.

There are variations. Model B is a membership operation, with staff paid in scrip. Model C trades in cash. Look at these models; then add your own.

Feature	Model		
	A	**B**	**C**
Storefront?	Yes	Yes	Yes
Membership required?	No	Yes	No
Membership fee or dues?	No	Yes	No
Get cash for selling?	No	No	Yes
Pay cash for buying?	No	No	Yes
Take what you need?	No	No	No
Method for setting value?	Appraiser	Appraiser	Appraiser
Paid staff?	No	Yes (scrip)	Yes (cash)
Items accepted?	All	All	All

*　　　*　　　*

The supermarket concept is too big for some people and for some communities in general. If it's too big, it's overwhelming, and it won't work. So many of the exchanges revert to types. There's one for clothes, specializing in infant and toddler ware. One for toys. One for sporting goods, especially for speedily-outgrown items like bicycles and skates. One for home video equipment and personal computers. One for general household items. One for hardware, concentrating on vintage goods appealing mainly to the connoisseur.

*　　　*　　　*

With the acquisition of an old post office truck for $500 in scrip, the thrift shop goes mobile. Paint the truck brightly, call it "Bargain Buggy," load the stuff in, drive it to the most remote neighborhoods, or where people don't get out. A traveling library of experienced goods.

*　　　*　　　*

On the radio: 9:00 a.m. is Telephone Trading Time. Call up with an item you'd like to trade or sell cheaply. Describe it and leave your phone number. Wait for the phone to ring.

In print: the *Barter and Trade Journal.* Free ads:

> Will trade Radio Shack 6 Channel, 5 watt, walkie talkie for — ducklings, chicks, poultry, meat, produce, honey, bricks, railroad ties, or open to suggestions. Call John at...

Sold monthly over the counter at convenience stores, and by subscription.

* * *

The regional barter fair looks funny. All kinds of people are sitting at tables and booths, but not selling anything. What is going on?

They're talking about things they would barter and trade. Make whatever deals you like. It's a yard sale without yard goods; a flea market without fleas.

On Town Day, the town sets aside the football field for the community bazaar, where anyone can trade goods or services.

Groups of families combine in yard sales. The town Yard Sale Coordinator posts this weekend's sale map.

* * *

The swap shop runs from an old church basement. The mechanics are simple: bring in the stuff you no longer need; take out the stuff you want; tidy up when necessary. The shop is open whenever the church is. No staff, no inventory. Voluntary communism at work, very big in the heartland.

* * *

People who are into food coupons and food refund offers form area clubs, and spend time trading by mail.

The bigger markets have slots for food coupon exchanges, alphabetically by type. Put in your unwanted coupons, take others away; basic trust applies. A store person cleans up and rearranges before closing, but once people get the hang of it things stay pretty neat.

Will there be a separate aisle for trading food itself?

* * *

When people in the professional service network got together, the first thing they did was pass around their business cards. Old Maid without the Black Queen. Everyone came away with a fistful. Once embossed, members could arrange their professional services — their legal, psychological, medical, dental, architectural, recreational, and financial services—more easily. Leaving the room, one trader wonders why the same concept could not work for the poor.

* * *

You can barter four ways: goods for goods, services for services, goods for services, and services for goods.

Service bartering is common: I'll shovel your walk if you'll feed my cat. Or I'll watch your child if you'll fix my roof. Or, I'll teach you BASIC if you'll teach me guitar. Learning exchanges like this one are especially popular.

These exchanges needn't be formal. Often, they're best left loose and spontaneous. I'll help you with your chores, silently assuming that some other time you'll help me with mine. Or, without fanfare, we can start keeping certain tools in a common place, for anyone to use. It's really a goal to arrive at such understandings, shared and unspoken.

* * *

But if more centralization and structure are called for, the Community Skills Exchange handles the arrangements. When someone calls and you give a service, you get time-based credits. When you call someone and draw on a service, you get debits. You have more obligation to participate, for every so often inactive accounts are cleared out. And you have a running balance that can't stay too far below zero too long. Credits and debits are phoned in on an honor system; but there's a central, non-honor-system coordinator who keeps track of the credit status of all accounts.

How do you make this simple and hassle-free? How do you keep people from getting ripped off? How do you get people to feel okay about asking for something? The answer is to start small, with a few clear rules, and then to grow slowly and carefully.

*   *   *

Go to the Loan Exchange if you want to borrow something. This spin-off attracts folks who don't want to release their goods outright, but who are willing to loan them temporarily or semi-permanently. You get a borrower's card, as at a library. Borrow the stuff for two weeks at a time; renew, with the owner's consent, for the duration. Sometimes the owner decides not to take the goods back, and they become part of the permanent collection.

Buy $X worth of materials at the building supply co-op and get Y hours free construction time. Or put in X hours of service and get $Y in free goods. Rebates for participation are given, in the most affordable currency.

Call the Interest File if you want a tennis partner, a camping companion, a fourth for bridge, an eighth for a square. This file is mostly avocational. You get names and numbers, and take it from there.

*   *   *

When an elderly neighbor broke a hip and needed to recuperate at home, neighbors took turns living at her house a few days at a time. They exchanged not just their services, but their whole selves.

*   *   *

The town exchanges its self with a like-named town in a faraway state. Every summer a delegation from one arrives for two weeks in the other, staying in private homes, but paying their own way. Guests see the sights and soak up the culture. Maybe they'll work at the plant. They bring ideas as presents and share them in writing, film, and public debate.

Another town looks forward to visitors from abroad. Another spends weekends with groups nearer home. Another has foreign pen pals — 500 letters per packet to save on postage.

*   *   *

Going somewhere? Post your destination on the community ride board near the town center. Traveling out of the area? Use the long-distance section. Or try the rides column in the local newspaper. Or call the local radio station — it does a community ride show once a week. Ratings are high, for people like to share travel and costs.

* * *

Businesses around here barter all the time now. Sometimes they keep score, other times not. The lines between barter and gift, favor and trade, fuzzy up.

Some of the bigger companies have barter managers. One former manager is a full-time barter broker, organizing and coordinating barter exchanges regionally. Two new Selectrics for a used pickup truck; a ton of fish for a tray of chips; fifty reams of paper for ten hours of landscaping. A company pays a yearly fee to get listed and to learn of items available. When it wants to trade, it calls the broker, who looks for a match. A little further down the line, type in what you're willing to trade, and watch the screen for what you can get back. Industrial computer dating.

* * *

Very quiet in the back alleys. The box division, the iron works, and the rubber factory have set out their trash. It waits....That's a VW camper rolling to a stop. Men and women hop out and look around. They load up with corrugated paper, metal parts, pieces of foam. They make their rounds, and head home full.

The van pulls up in front of what looks like a store. It is — a free store of industrial scrap. Teachers come by and pick up materials for their kids. Poor parents find stocking stuffers. Artists find collages.

In this factory outlet, supply-side economics is practiced. Industrial recycling is five days a week.

* * *

Tuesday, garbage day, dawn's early light. Junk harvesters on the prowl. That old chair still has springs breathing. Maybe some spare parts in this clock radio. What's that over there, a toaster oven? Another full truckload.

Junk harvesting is common practice now, a sideline for some, a way of life for others. No stigma attached. Some depositors go so far as to tie red tags on the choicest items. Bold crews search the dumpsters. This is anonymous exchange, unrequited. Garbage crews are happy; less trash to haul.

The big stuff winds up at the town dump, where the DPW is kind enough to arrange it by category. The Dumpmaster sets out directional signs, fresh flowers, and picnic tables. New arrivals stay a month before getting trashed for good.

* * *

One harvester usually arrives before the others. She's a dealer. Takes the good stuff down to her shop, dusts it off, fixes it up, sorts it on shelves. All kinds of garbage down there which is too down-and-out to sell, but too good to throw away, or so she thinks. She calls her place Community Yard Sale. People come down and take things home, pay in loose change, maybe add items of their own. She's retired, not in it for the money, but rather for the sentiment and the preservation of material culture.

* * *

No, we rarely use money here. Money is an instrument of mass society; we're in the post-monetary era now. Most of the time, we use tokens instead. One thousand per year are given to each man, woman, and child.

You're right, you can't buy anything with them, in the traditional sense. But you can exchange them for whatever you like. You have to remember, though, that these tokens are good only in our community. The next town over is more primitive than we are, and still uses gold stars, I think.

We're proud of our token economy here. We've begun to create our own economic system.

* * * * *

*

*   *   *

*

Wally the driver greets people climbing on to his bus. (''Wally's Bus'' is painted on the outside.) ''Good morning! Fine day, isn't it?'' He tells funny stories. At the next red light he turns to his riders and says, ''How about a few songs to put us all in the right mood?'' Song sheets fan down the aisle. Forty-eight seated passengers and a few standees sing, ''Oh, What a Beautiful Mornin' '' as the bus rolls downtown.

*

*   *   *

*

street life

Here comes the tap dancing class down the street again. Concrete's a good tapping surface, but God they make a lot of noise.

*　　*　　*

The town pays streetwalkers. A rough cross between cop and hooker, town crier thrown in. They walk the streets pure and simple. Their job is to pass out information, help people who need help, control people who need control, watch out for things suspicious, solve little problems, and dispense kind words.

*　　*　　*

The streetwalkers have routes like buses. Route 3 starts at the information kiosk, then goes by the outdoor bulletin board, past the photomural and the statues of heroes, near the sidewalk tables where people sit absorbed in each other, around the public computer alcove, through the Japanese garden and the pocket park, across from where the newspaper is posted, alongside the water sculpture, and then back to the beginning.

*　　*　　*

The streetwalkers keep logs. Here's an hour's sample:

...Balloon lady is out of change. Give her some from my change dispenser. Will pop into the bank and pick up some coin rolls on my way back.

...Older man trips on curb. Help him up. Doesn't want medical assistance. Looks shaken, but okay.

...Kids visiting town want street directions. Give them a neighborhood map from my pouch. Almost out, better go back and get more.

...*That* kid looks pretty little to be out on the street alone. What is she, maybe four or five? But then again a lot of kids travel the streets alone here because they and their parents feel safe and secure.

She's carrying groceries back from the store. I'll say hi to her.
"How're you doing, honey? Want a hand?"
"Get out of my way, mister." Tough little kid.

...The street musician wants me to hear her new number, Villa-Lobos' Prelude #5. Sounds great, but ask her to turn down the amplifier a little.

...Who is that masked man? Oh, the bookstore is at it again. A sign in the window offers a free book to anyone coming in wearing a costume.

...Do I know where the Lions Club meets? Yes, I do.

...Man relates complex story about allegedly missing veterans benefits. I know a little veterans law by now, and think I can help him out. Tell him where to go, who to see and what to say at the Veterans Office.

...Tell those youngsters riding bikes to get them off the sidewalk.

...Stop by older woman's house and ring the doorbell to make sure she is okay.

...Uh-oh, one of my jacket buttons comes off. Lucky the clothing store is just a few steps away. They make a practice of sewing buttons and mending small rips on the spot and while you wait. No charge, of course. Good business policy.

…Pick an apple off the fruit cart. Drop a coin in the box, as the owner's not there right now.

…I have a joke for Joe the barber. Joe asks me if I could drop this envelope off at the phone company.

…Most meters on this street show time expired. Make note to tell meter supervisor to check street more often.

…Couple approaches, speaks no English. Language sounds like one I never heard. Take out my pocket card with "Can I Help You?" in 40 languages, and they point to the one that's theirs. Then by thumbing through my pocket directory, I give them linguistic kin to call.

…Make personal and off-the-record recommendation of a reliable and reasonably-priced plumber.

…This one's a school class on a field trip. Teacher wants to make appointment to have class watch me on my rounds. Next week, probably. A lot of times I have company, usually people from other towns who want to see how I work. But right now it's time for lunch.

* * *

In another town, the streetwalkers are all cop, doing what cops used to do. In another, they are retired cops. In another, they are young parents with kids in strollers. In another, they are civil service grade 12. In another, they are retired or unretired volunteers.

* * *

There's Tawny the cat, drinking at the pet fountain. Dogs and cats get thirsty, you know. Tawny is a street cat, who spends a while in one place and moves on to another. She's the town mascot.

* * *

In the agora, people cluster in twos and threes and tens and twenties. They meet and talk, do business upstanding, for the agora is designed for maximum words per square foot. News is exchanged; invitations are tendered and accepted. People flow between groups, in unplanned dance.

* * *

The selectmen will meet outside at noon today. The meeting is open to everyone, has to be. Most public meetings are open-air, with earth as boardroom table and chair. Sitting on the grass is an equalizer. Sitting in the sun saves fuel. On the edges, small boys and girls will sell lemonade and peanut butter and jelly and cheese sandwiches, and toss salads with house dressing.

* * *

Shopkeepers and office workers take their lunch hours to listen to a robed man talk of beauty, the good life, and what is true. He asks many questions, yet hardly ever seems satisfied with answers received. He keeps probing. The atmosphere is charged.

* * *

Off duty, the streetwalker notices little kids sitting under a tree listening to an old woman. She is telling stories about when she was young, adding a few of her own. Imagination and truth blend together. Today the old woman is culture-bearer and day care center. The kids are rapt. They will sit until dark, and they will remember.

* * *

In the streets, there are street vendors and pushcart peddlers, fortune tellers and gossip mongers, jugglers and child magicians, a clown polishing her act.

In the streets, there are wandering minstrels and roller skaters, sound trucks and amateur hours, inner observers and happiness dealers, kids playing tag.

In the streets there are pony rides.

In the streets, there's a speaker's corner, with posted schedule and rules. There are white-gloved and helmeted people on platforms directing traffic on hourly tours.

In the streets, there is entertainment for the theater-goer, humility for the proud, solace for the lonely, a continuous and embracing support system.

* * *

In the heat of the afternoon, a couple in plain view kisses passionately smack on the lips.

* * *

In the streets, there are eyes to give you identity and affirmation, and if you want to provoke it, attention and interest, and if you want to provoke some more, command and evaluation, which is the price you pay for stepping out. In the streets, you are street life, giving recognition and protection to others simply by your presence.

* * *

In the evening when the day dies down, the town turns out to the square. The crowd moves in broad circles, following the *paseo*. Eyes are on bright. Mating dance and community renewal are embedded within. This is human ritual.

Balladeers appear, playing softly. The strollers dissolve into small groups and sit quietly listening after the music fades away.

* * *

"Now the town is dusk. Each cobble, donkey, goose and gooseberry street is a thoroughfare of dusk; and dusk and ceremonial dust, and night's first darkening snow, and the sleep of birds, drift under and through the live dusk of this place of love."

* * *

The life of the agora flows onto the side streets. Everyone's a street land lord or lady. The lords and ladies come out to mingle with the members of their kingdom; or they hold court from their top steps and watch the pageantry go by.

* * *

Along the side street, residents at round tables, leafing through newspapers, doing some sewing, catching some rays, chatting with each other and passersby. Yes, the tables take up room. No, we built them ourselves. Yes, it makes the block unique and once the tables were there everyone wanted them to stay.

A local carpenter builds benches, planters, love seats, ornamental signposts, better than those the city has ordered, and sets them outside on his own as a gift. Eventually, the city will change its supplier.

*　　　*　　　*

Step one — the corner grocery starts selling takeout coffee and donuts. Step two — a few stools to sit on while eating and drinking. Step three — homemade pastries brought in by the baker lady up the street. Step four — try putting a few tables out back. Step five — add collapsible umbrellas for hot sun. Step six — add newspapers. Why not? It doesn't hurt business. Step seven — chess, checkers, dominoes, available on request. Step eight — bring the tables out front. That's how the mom and pop grocery became the sidewalk cafe.

*　　　*　　　*

When it's winter and cold, there are advantages to a climate-controlled shopping mall. The mall becomes main street. Street life moves inside.

After hours, the stores close down, but the mall stays open. A pickup foam-rubber soccer game starts at one end, an evening fashion show at the other. There are sight readings, prayer meetings, college classes. Later on a dance band moves in — great acoustics — and the dancers party till dawn.

*　　　*　　　*

Streets change their names to suit the times. Ours is Easy Street. There's Penny Lane, Yellow Brick Road, Sunshine Square.

*　　　*　　　*

Clothes are looser and more colorful since more people have taken up home sewing and pattern design. The street is full of patchwork and gypsies.

Some wear audible clothing, bells jingling softly as they walk. The streetwalkers in particular are portable wind chimes.

Dress customs loosen as well. The reference librarian wears a T-shirt: "I'm a Stubborn Old Goat." The bank teller's sun visor says it's better in the Bahamas.

*   *   *

In front of the food market, once a week, local cooks spoon out their best to the curious and the starving as long as it lasts. They are mostly showing off. But the tasters also vote, and the market takes an option to buy the goods of the high vote-getters in quantity and to sell them from its shelves.

*   *   *

The Cast in Concrete theater is getting ready to perform. Today is Ibsen's *Enemy of the People*, Act I. (Act II next week.) They will go 30-40 minutes, and pass the hat. They move from place to place, intermixing with other street arts groups as part of a twilight performance series. They are in repertory, specializing in classics, but with occasional premieres.

A schedule is posted: this week a fado singer, a gospel choir, a Goliard poet, a slide show maker, standup comedy, modern dance. Different genres every day, rotating through neighborhoods, in a Latin square.

For today's events on the street, check the pegboard. You're doing something you want other people to know about, post it for the proper time.

*   *   *

The streetwalker stops to feel the texture of the streets. In a 50-yard radius, there are people walking, running, sitting, and lying down; hurrying and sauntering; arguing and meditating; sunbathing and stretching; whistling, calling, buying, selling, eating, playing; crossing the street, eyeing each other, striking up conversations, moving freely; reading, riding, hiding, seeking.

Suddenly the scene is powerfully familiar, as if viewed centuries ago. If only he could paint. He wonders where he's seen this tapestry before.

*   *   *   *   *

economic development

The private and public sector lunch club is meeting today to review pie slices and plan joint projects.

Here's how they will combine: The private sector agrees to set sail. It takes the risk. It puts up most of the capital, builds the facility, hires the employees, and creates the product. It is ultimately responsible for success or failure.

The public sector will help arrange for financing. It supplies technical assistance. It provides tax credits for starting up, especially in poor neighborhoods, especially if neighborhood residents are hired, especially if they are youth. It leverages the capital and cushions the risk, like a good broker.

The two sectors will leave together, each thinking how much it admires the other.

* * *

Graduation day is coming up at High Technology University. It was a bold stroke for the computer company to plan a university of its own, no less bold to persuade its competitors to join in. HTU is fully accredited now; its graduates command top dollar. The state was just as wise to acquire the land for the university park, which is where commencement exercises will be held.

Meanwhile, classes start tomorrow at the state business college, a part-time program for small-time entrepreneurs long on drive and short on experience. No degree, no grades in this version, but certificates of completion based on demonstrated skills. The school makes money, because tuition is ten percent of first-year profits. But even without tuition, the state figures that the program is cost-effective, in attracting many new business persons who will serve the community.

* * *

"For us, service is one of the most important criteria we have in choosing what we do with our lives....The reason that business has such a potential for being rewarding is that it is a very special way that people can serve each other."

* * *

The State Industrial Council, jointly financed, is a clearing house for new business projects and ideas. It matches venture capital with ventures. It solicits both. It calls up specialists and asks for their help. It calls up small businesses and asks how they are doing.

Local groups may apply to the Chamber of Commerce and Social Welfare. The Chamber meets regularly with residents to respond to their needs. Its Social Awareness Committee adopts hometown social service programs and encourages local companies to do the same. Peer pressure is a specialty. Its theme this year — "Put your money where your house is."

* * *

In a frozen neighborhood, one merchant broke the ice. The merchant's association thus organized set a budget, designed a logo, hung up signs, strung up banners, built a bus shelter, took out bus ads, printed coupon books, hired costumed handbill carriers, planted some flowers, extended their hours, cleaned their facades, swept their streets, held sidewalk sales, put on shows, sponsored baseball teams, purchased a van, recruited a band, hid some treasure, promoted a fair, ran a coloring contest, exhibited window art, gave out a scholarship, and lit up for Christmas. That was the first year.

.   .   .

The Dedham Diner has to move down the road, but has no money for moving expenses, and who in hell will finance moving a diner? So you go to your customers and borrow from them. Promissory notes at $100 a pop, redeemable in cash or in store credit with a bonus. The diner sells 50, takes the $5000 and moves. Here is a people's loan association, trusting in a successful business.

The ad hoc association can become a permanent revolving loan fund. The loan fund can become a credit union. The credit union can become a bank. The bank can be formal or informal, physical or spiritual, inside or beside the law. Mindset is the charter ingredient.

Local banks loan mostly inside the community. They set aside low-interest funds for new community projects. Imagination is mandated. The low-cost loan applications are put out for public comment; comments and decisions are kept up front.

Some banks specialize. The First Shepherd's Bank, for example, specializes in Christian causes, and draws on biblical authority. Most depositors tithe. The tithers vote on directors, and the directors vote on causes. And so this bank finances one of the most active social service systems in the country, both through loans and direct distribution of profits.

The First Latin Bank is not too far behind. The Veterans and Libertarian Banks are in the planning stages. The area socialists wonder what their bank would look like. At First Idealist, you pay back what you can.

.   .   .

A voluntary simplicity group meets regularly. Its path veers far from economic growth. It meets to discuss sharing more and spending less, but, just as important, to support each other for leading lives which go against the norm of increasing one's income and material standard of living.

* * *

The community development corporation has inspired neighborhood economic plans, required neighborhood impact reviews, and restored block power to the blocks. But now, tarnished by success, it realizes that economic development starts from within. So the people's business school opens up. The students learn self-confidence, problem-solving, cash flow management, and community consciousness. They learn too about how wealth is apportioned in our society and how prosperity is tied to its redistribution.

But the emphasis is largely on formation and refinement of personal economic goals. The corporation grasps that community development begins with software, inside the brain. If self-development comes first, community development will follow.

* * * * *

government

One town leader said that if the town really believed in democracy, then all people ought to be able to vote on all town issues. "But how can this be done?" he was asked. "They have telephones, don't they?" And so government by telephone was born.

Now when there's a significant community issue (we still have to fix the criteria), we announce it in the local paper and over radio and cable, and we have a minimum two-week period of debate, unless it's an emergency and we have to take a vote immediately.

Then there's voting day. Should we approve the school bond issue? Should we pass the zoning bylaws? Should we merge with regional transit? Each voter calls in his or her choice to the election office. The office crosses each name off the list, and tallies the votes. Then you have your policy decision.

The way it works is that you don't actually have to express an opinion yourself. You may feel that your elected representatives are the best ones to vote on this particular issue, and you would rather let them decide. In that case, you call in "abstain," which gives them a proxy. The only requirement is that more than 50 percent of the electorate has to cast ballots — abstentions included — before any decision becomes final.

Granted, it's possible to falsify. We can check by using social security numbers. If that doesn't work, we can go to voice codes, with voice-code screening at election central. Or we can try two-way cable television, like the QUBE system in use already. Or here's another idea: for about $25, we can give each registered voter a portable transmitter, with "yes," "no," and "abstain" buttons, maybe with a page-call feature. The voter just pushes a button, and the signals come in on unique frequencies to a computerized receiver, which sorts them out and counts them up. Sometimes you have to keep abreast of the new technology, even though there's start-up expense. But these high-tech people in town ought to be able to contribute something, right? The system will eventually save money down at the election office; meanwhile we can amortize the rest of the cost off the tax rate.

*　　*　　*

Another townsperson says that all of this is foolish. Sure you want people to vote, but skip the technology. When you are ready for voting, have people come down to the amphitheater, or let them gather in the streets. They won't be driving then, so don't worry about the traffic. Give them a half-hour to inspect the goods, like previews at auctions. Then vote, by acclamation. Direct democracy, yes, but keep it simple.

*　　*　　*

To make this or any democracy work well, you have to boost the franchise:

To begin with, town elections and most other votes are on weekends, when people have more time.

The high schools give voting a big push, and hold voter sign-ups in the guidance office and on Registration Day in senior history class.

Anyone can become a deputy registrar by passing a one-evening course and becoming duly certificated: you can then take your clipboard around town and sign up anyone on the spot.

The registrars have contests: winners get steak knives.

The League of Women and Men Voters has a free transportation service and sends out 18th birthday cards with return coupons enclosed.

Voters with perfect five-year records get to choose between a $10 credit off their municipal income tax or $20 worth of lottery tickets.

Parents have an extra vote for each non-voting minor child in their custody, limit of two. Isn't that right? They control their children's money and their personal lives, so why not their votes? This also helps keep kids interested in town affairs, and parents on their toes.

Children in fact can vote in local elections whenever they go down unaccompanied to the clerk's office and sign an affidavit swearing they now consider themselves responsible citizens and claiming their voting rights.

. . .

During the 1964 presidential campaign, I was a deputy registrar in California, sitting at a shopping center, signing up whomever came along. An older woman approached me and asked if I could go over to her car and register her father who didn't walk very well. Sure. There was a really old man in the car, 96 at the time. He said he had voted in every election through when he was 92. When he was 94, he got sick, missed the election, and so according to state law his registration expired. But now at 96 he's feeling better, and wants to register again.

Will we give him an extra vote for age? For determination?

. . .

Some places, co-candidates for office are coming in fashion. Families run for one slot together. Tasks are split, and kids help out.

Some places, *running* for office is out of style. On election day, you just vote for the people you want. Those with the most votes are supposed to serve.

Other places, that's a little too scattered, and people prefer the full town meeting, where anyone can speak, and it's one person, one vote. But sometimes the group is just too big, in which case the representative town meeting is the most popular form. The town meeting members usually come from election districts, or precincts, and this usually means a precinct association, another strong membership group for those who live here.

*   *   *

When the budget ax kept falling, executive functions shifted to volunteer committees. Ongoing committees made up of interested townspeople sit on top of most town issues. (When a new issue comes up, an ad hoc committee is formed which lasts as long as the issue does.) Members of both kinds of committees are generally nominated and appointed, though sometimes self-anointed.

Meetings are publicized and open to all. Anyone who shows up can talk and vote. The voters thus become those there at that time, which usually means a core of regulars plus a few who are particularly interested.

The status of membership is loose, and deliberately so; decisions are made by the people who want to make them. Formal votes are rarely taken, though, for the committees try to reach decisions by consensus, following the group dynamics principles in their government handbooks.

*   *   *

Government in another town works by rotation. Names are drawn from the census, much as for jury duty. Some jobs rotate daily: flag raiser, night clerk, park worker, crossing guard. For others you get an invitation in the mail, usually to serve on one of the standing or ad hoc committees. Details and time commitments are spelled out; assignments are generally for a year. You can refuse, but there is social pressure to accept, for service is part of being a citizen, and people are educated that way from grade school up. The community service you give is officially recorded and totalled. And on Town Day, those who've provided the most service during the year are publicly honored.

Elsewhere, service credits are distributed. That is, if you put 100 hours in, you get 100 credits, valid any time in the next year. An ambulance call, for example, is worth 40 credits at current rates of exchange. Yearly trash collection costs you 80 credits; a library card 10; an adult education course 25. You can cash in your credits this way, or trade them around, or sell them on the open white market. You can get services without credits too, though it's mostly cash and carry.

But in some other places, town service is a formal obligation of residence. The tax reductions once given out have now been cancelled. The argument used is that the town is like a cooperative, and so requires a cooperative effort. To keep the benefits you get from the town, you have to give some benefits back.

*   *   *

The holiday catalog came in the mail today, four-color this time. You can buy a doorknob on the new administration building for $5, or a library book for $15. A street sign will set you back $100, while monkey bars for the playground are $500 this year. Other holiday gifts: a fire fighter's helmet; a year's supply of paper clips, slides for the school microscope, some teeth for the Jaws of Life, batons for the drum majorettes. Send your check to the town. You get your name in the paper, a sense of community pride, an engraving on the gift (optional, if $100 or more), and of course a chance to read the book, heed the sign, or see the majorettes in action.

But if you can't give money to the community, you can give the gift of time. You can affirm:

I, _____ , hereby
donate
_____100_____50_____25_____10_____Other
hours of service to the community for the _____
calendar year, subject to the following conditions
(check one below):
_____With service limited to the following
areas(s):

_____With service preferred in the following
areas:

_____With service consisting of whatever work the community deems necessary, consistent with physical capacity and training.

Comments:

_____   _____
(signed)   (date)

You can also *barter* with the community, by making arrangements through the community barter officer.

*   *   *

The municipal garage sale is held in the town yard. Free punch, and half price after 4:00. Not much for the connoisseur, but mostly down-home stuff like a couple of extra rakes, sacks of tar patch, miscellaneous auto parts, leftover office supplies, etc. No dealers, please.

*   *   *

The mayor is available to anyone during her public office hours. Drop in if you like, or better, make an appointment with the receptionist.

The day mayor meets the evening mayor coming up the steps. The evening mayor says good night to the night mayor. The city needs three mayors, for it's open 24 hours a day, and people have needs during each one of them. City hall stays open around the clock, like the convenience store it is.

There's also an open logbook in the city hall lobby. Here's the place for you to write your compliments, complaints, and fantasies about local government. Write on the left side. The day mayor takes the book home and writes back on the right. Department heads and school principals by now have started logbooks of their own. This makes for ongoing dialogue.

*   *   *

The town manager flags a bus and leaves Town A for Town B. On his arrival, he will become manager of B. Tomorrow he'll head over to C. He circuit-rides. The towns share him, buying his services jointly, divvying him up.

The town figures it can't afford a lot of things on its own, but maybe it could if it chipped in with its neighbors. So now there are regional associations of communities which time-share a computer for their payroll, billing, and data-processing needs. They pool some fire, police, and ambulance equipment and vehicles. They each use the same management consultant. The dog officer knows no boundaries, nor does the health inspector. The communities have made up separate equipment inventories, and have started meeting to explore what could be bartered, or loaned, or commonly owned.

The town figures why not use modern management techniques, even if our budget is limited? So they hire and split an outside evaluator, to make sure the services they're getting are useful, cost effective, and as promised. She visits programs periodically, helps them form objectives, and gets them to set standards for evaluating their own work. She says it's much better in the long run that programs evaluate and correct themselves than have an outsider do it for them. Her goal is to make evaluation second nature.

The towns share a grantsperson. Two unforeseen results: 1. The grantsperson, through research and field work, has found additional ways to combine resources; 2. Several winning joint applications have been submitted, which might not have won had the applicants applied singly.

*   *   *

The big city has little city halls, branch offices in the neighborhoods, performing most of the big hall functions. Government moves out closer to the people.

This does cost some money. When government can't swing it, government itself circuit-rides, spends several hours per week per church basement and shopping center, or sets bridge tables on the street.

Some little city halls go mobile, and wind their way like ice cream men. On reaching marked stops, they jingle their bells and wait for customers.

In the country, the little county seat is the rear of a jeep. It rattles into all the towns of the district once a week, and will make house calls in emergencies. On the way back, it beeps hello to the local congressional office, heading in the opposite direction.

•   •   •

Lowell, Mass., early morning: The congressman's father, born in Greece, sends some baklava down to the local office for sweet beginnings.

•   •   •

The neighborhood association gets pledges from the city department heads that they will visit the neighborhood at least once a month in person, to talk to the people and take a look around. The neighborhood looks forward to these walking and talking tours — it's nice to have the chief of police or the traffic engineer over at your place every once in a while. It's good for visibility, for communication, for accountability, for staying in touch with the territory, and for human scale.

Scorecard is a watchdog group chosen by the neighborhood associations. Members grade government performance, and any other public performance they have a mind to. Scorecard holders walk the streets, and record police responses, cleanliness levels, code violations, fire waiting times. They grade on preset criteria, worked out in advance with the department in question. They put out a quarterly report card with numbers. Their grades mean money. They are bribed and threatened, which is a good sign. They are tough and controversial, and meant to be. A lot of people don't like them, and partly for that reason they are going to be around for a while.

•   •   •

The town gave up on the property tax long ago, and went directly to a graduated municipal tax on income, with unearned income, as from property, being taxed at twice the earned rate. Home rule applies, with voter consent.

The next step was computing local taxes directly from state tax forms. The step after that was to allow each taxpayer partial choice of beneficiary. Take ten percent of your eggs and choose your baskets. Bring home the meaning of public service.

Meanwhile, the constitutionality of a neighborhood tax is pending in the courts.

*   *   *

One of the most productive line items in the town budget is a $10,000 fund for small grants to neighborhood and community groups and even individual citizens. You can apply for up to $2,000 for any community program you want. A volunteer board reviews the proposals; innovation is stressed. Even $1,000 can go a long way, and can get something off the ground that couldn't have risen before.

*   *   *

Kansas: The Community Resource Act:

"...Community resource programs are a means for people throughout the state to share their skills and knowledge with one another...and thereby to perpetuate the concept of volunteerism and enhance the quality of life in Kansas; and therefore it is in the public interest of the state, and it is the purpose of this act, to provide financial assistance for community resource programs..."

*   *   *

Minnesota: Several corporations organize themselves into the Five Percent Club, each pledging to give the maximum five percent in corporate contributions allowed by law. They recruit other corporate members, so that they can find worthwhile community projects. They leverage their money with matching provisions and challenge grants. They would challenge local government itself.

*   *   *

Cambridge, Mass.: City employees are under a lot of pressure. The massage company has a trial arrangement to give back rubs at lunch. About ten minutes should keep folks loose for the rest of the day. Will there be a carryover effect?

*   *   *

Boy Scout Troop 513 has this year's contract to keep up the parks. The community thought it might get better performance if it hired people who really wanted to see the work get done. So many services once provided by municipal employees are now sent out for bid and contract.

The Friends of Libraries do filing and shelving. Healthy Fun Incorporated runs the recreation programs. The football team hauls the trash and will use its pay to buy new uniforms. The Sewer Rats look after the infrastructure.

The city supplies the basics — police, fire, ambulance, schools, water — that's about it. The neighborhood councils get cash, "block grants" for the rest, divided up by population. Each council then decides how much it wants to appropriate for each service, and how it wants them delivered. It can hire neighborhood employees, or contract out to other groups, or contract back with the city if it prefers. Services are based on local need. Management can be local too. The neighborhood can get in about as deep as it wants to.

·   ·   ·

The sun sets tonight on the Board of Assessors. Also on the Council on Aging and the Youth Commission. It's the end of the budget submission period, and unless a new request is submitted with full justification for each item, starting from zero, the program at least technically goes out of business. Well, not really, most of the time, but a few programs have actually been darkened by sunset provisions. Programs don't have tenure; they must be reborn. Every budget cycle is an opportunity for renewal and rebirth.

·   ·   ·

Each department sets objectives for the coming year. Quantitative, measurable targets, performance goals, theses posted on the doors and in the press. Next year's budget rests on this year's goal performance. The same goes for the performances of individuals within the departments. One of the most meritorious things about these merit reviews is that they are actually done.

·   ·   ·

In the Office of Rewards and Punishments, the staff look at their wall charts and decide how best to apply social reinforcement principles on a community level.

• • •

The social service officer coordinates those services around town. He convenes the monthly inter-agency meeting. He administers the mini-grant program. He brings social science expertise to hard-nosed planning decisions. He signs off on social impact statements, stating how physical planning projects will affect social quality of life. He knows where grant money is and how to dig it up. He is a matchmaker who brings people together, an organizer who establishes intra- and inter-community collaborations. He knows who is doing what, and what ought to start, and what can be trimmed, and he isn't shy. In general, he earns his pay.

• • •

The sanitation truck rolls past town hall. "Hey, we're one short today. Who can help?" A couple of bored clerks hop on. Town workers are supposed to cover for each other. Don't they all work for the same cause?

• • • • •

energy

Among the contest entries to name the new municipal wind-power station were Inherit the Wind, Breath of Life, Breeze and I, Mill the Wind, Windmills of Your Mind, Huff and Puff, Breezing Along, Sky Power, Air Force, and Windy City. They settled on Airway.

Once the community got the mindset that it could generate its own energy and didn't have to rely on outside power, the rest was relatively easy. Wind, after all, is renewable. It took some technical expertise to build the main facility, install the generator, and run power lines, but the people drew on the engineers in the town who had suggested the idea in the first place. In not too long, rival home windmill kits with optional central hookups will be coming on the market. It will be fun to sell electricity back to the utility company.

The people realized they could insulate their houses up to the R-100th factor, till the Fiberglas oozed out the chimney. But they understood that the point was for the community to become energy-independent. Energy conservation is great, but energy generation is what makes conservation possible.

*   *   *

Another group of engineers with a little hydrological background takes a day off to walk along the banks of the river once taken for granted, noting the strength of the current.

*　　*　　*

You can come to the community forest and haul away dead wood during wood-hunting season in the fall. And you can cut a standard cord of your own within a target area. The Department of Natural Resources stakes the boundaries and checks the operation. You bring your own chain saw and pickup truck.

*　　*　　*

The home-made still out back turns out fuel-grade ethanol. Start with soybeans or corn. Process them through a cooker, an alcohol fermenter, and two still tanks. Leave the beer tank alone for later. Take the ethanol from the dehydration tank, mix with nine parts gasoline, and you have gasohol for your car. The U.S. government shows you how to do this in words and pictures.

*　　*　　*

Solar barnraisings take place most Sundays of the year; consult your local newspaper for details. Men and women gather outside a house, donate their muscles to lift a neighbor's solar panels into place, and help with other installations as needed. Slides of finished work convince others to join; they learn while they are doing. Soon, their own homes will be ready, and they'll get the help they need.

It took a while before the town followed the example of its citizens and started to put solar equipment on its own buildings. But now, it's lovely to work in the solar office complex. It's delightful to swim in the solar gymnasium. Meanwhile, tomatoes and peppers grow in the solar greenhouse, unmindful of snowdrifts, confident of endless summer.

Most homes come equipped with outdoor solar dryers. In late winter, some financially-strapped communities practice solar snowplowing.

*　　*　　*

The electric company decides to become a public utility, and holds elections for its board. Ballots are mailed with the electric bill. Each month offers checks and balances.

The company gives back bonus bucks for the installation of energy-efficient appliances. These are coupons, good for reductions on future utility bills, which come in various types and denominations, its Solar T-Bills among the most popular.

The utility rate structure itself has been turned upside down. The price per energy unit gets costlier the more energy you use, not cheaper. What's more, there's a menu-full of rate structures you can buy into, just as with the telephone. You can buy bare-bones service, for a bare-bones price. You can get time-of-use rates, where you pay less for using power at off times of the day. You can change rates according to the season. You can order à la carte or table d'hôte. And you can choose conservation-incentive rates, which give you rebates for reducing your total consumption by fixed percentages from last year's.

*   *   *

Consumers came to realize they would use less energy if they knew more facts. They said to the utility company we can barely read your meters, and we rarely read them voluntarily. The company said you are right, and soon arranged for digital meters with cumulative and resettable features, like odometers on cars, and put them in first floor wall panels.

Half the new customers got the new meters automatically. Half the old customers could buy them for a modest one-time fee. Half of both digital and dial groups got trended printouts on their bills. Random assignment applied. The company's researchers studied usage patterns for each subgroup, computed average payback times, published their results, suggested policies accordingly, and helped colleagues follow suit.

*   *   *

Materials about conservation aren't hard to find, what with energy audits, media write-ups, library displays and all. But each year the town sponsors an energy fair, where new techniques are demonstrated, questions answered, and people wanting to swap information or labor on home projects can get together.

Sign-ups are taken for the fuel oil co-op. Storm windows now can be ordered in bulk. Burner service is sold at a group rate. Tours are given of the geothermal home.

Portland, Oregon: The city ordinance states that houses sold after 1984 must have cost-effective energy-conservation materials up to a specified standard. Otherwise, unless owner compensates buyer, it's illegal to sell.

* * *

School children learn about energy conservation in class and practice it by insulating a model house, weather-stripping the classroom windows, wearing thermal socks, and circling the outside with caulking guns.

The kids also resolve to keep a sharp ear out for leaky faucets since the "Don't Be a Drip" water conservation campaign. During the campaign, the Water Department distributed free shower flow controllers to each student, picking up the tab itself, putting the cost under capital outlay.

* * *

At home, we make a New Year's resolution to engage in personal energy conservation. Life is tough, that's all the more reason. We said we'll try to honor each moment and to worry less. No more running for buses. More walking in the woods. Only a reasonable number of outside commitments. Grace before meals, family talk after. Less waste motion in our own lives.

* * *

While in Bermuda, the vacationing couples recalled how they got there. They belonged to a neighborhood entered in the town-wide energy-saving competition. The idea was that all entrants would for a month use as little externally-generated energy as they healthfully could.

Neighborhood meter readings were taken before and during and charted in town hall, alongside thermometers showing each neighborhood's progress. Pep rallies marked the weekly postings.

Many candlelight dinners were eaten that month. People gathered around fires at each other's houses, held adult pajama parties, and shared each other's warmth. In retrospect, it was enriching, and it was fun.

At the end, awards were made in both Least Absolute Usage and Greatest Percentage Decrease categories. Individual winners were chosen by drawing from the winning neighborhood participants. The town paid for the trip, reasoning that the net energy savings more than made up for the air and hotel bills.

* * *

There was a by-product, which was that energy consumption in the community would from now on always be visible. The town had learned two powerful lessons for modifying behavior: (1) create group goals; (2) provide knowledge of results.

* * * * *

trash

San Francisco: Garbage men and women, dressed in serapes, swing the cans and sing sea chanteys.

*   *   *

When the townspeople decided to get tough on trash:

They required fast food restaurants and convenience stores to pay for putting trash baskets outside their premises.

They put wastebaskets with flip-top lids in the buses, near the doors.

They decorated their trash cans with hippo mouths and ruby lips. They emblazoned the cans with day-glo colors and "Stuff it Here" logos. They affixed bull's-eyes and hidden tape recorders which said thank you very much.

They blended other trash baskets with the landscaping so they wouldn't be too conspicuous.

They made sure there was a trash barrel on every block. When some of them started to disappear, they bought barrels with round bottoms and chained them to lampposts.

They passed a bottle bill in the town when the state wouldn't.

They passed a pooper-scooper law and sent the junior dog officer out to enforce it. The fine for first violation was three certified hours on pooper-scooper patrol.

They set up special dog runs for pets, which dog owners agreed to maintain on a regular basis.

They put up signs: "A cleaner town is up to me."

They began a dirty pictures campaign through the newspaper so that people would feel ashamed. They put loose trash they collected on exhibit in the glass cases in the library. They dumped the rest of it in front of town hall so that people would get mad.

They taught civic responsibility in the schools, and found useful work for kids on detention.

They passed an ordinance requiring merchants to sweep their sidewalks every morning.

The merchants association bought I'm Picking the Town Clean t-shirts and spent Saturday till sunset picking the last breadcrumb out of the town center.

They said that trash was treasure and had Treasure Hunt Day, when the treasure you brought in was weighed and exchanged for ice cream cones at the sponsoring soda shoppe.

They started cleanathons where people pledged cash for trash which kept several street kids in business for a while.

They changed their minds a little about the local religious cult when in flowing robes and vinyl sacks their members picked up every gum wrapper in a one-mile radius.

They contracted with neighborhoods to maintain the landscape and gave power mowers to the people.

They sponsored a clean block poster contest.

The blocks themselves established pickup committees and semi-annual cleanup days. They appointed block sanitation captains, and on streets where there were lots of apartment buildings, enlisted apartment dwellers at lesser rank.

They bought push brooms and trash barrels on wheels through their block associations and said to the street sweepers on rotation you can also serve as informal block patrols.

They went out disguised as bag men and women and filled their bags with garbage.

They asked all pet owners to keep their animals inside and sucked up everything else in sight with their power vacuums.

They sentenced graffiti artists to paint over their own handiwork, but also set aside graffiti areas as free-spray zones.

They tagged abandoned cars and towed them after a week to the public junkyard.

They designated special days for garbage pickup of large items — appliances, furniture, organic matter — and proposed specials of the month.

They pushed back garbage collection time for an hour to encourage trash picking.

They trucked their trash to the Whole Earth Recycling Center, which used to be the dump. They paid cash on the barrel for properly sorted newspapers, glass containers, autumn leaves, and computer cards.

They started a wholly-owned subsidiary, called Urban Ore, to specialize in new, as contrasted with re-use. They said bring us your scrap metal and we'll give you machine parts. Bring us your cooking oil, we'll give you fuel.

They started a hotline to report abuses, and deputized citizens to issue summonses.

They fined litterbugs an automatic $10 and gave second-time violators enforcement duty and third-time offenders a broom.

They gave lunch to the sanitation crews to thank them for their help.

They called themselves paper tigers and dressed the part. A paper drops: the people hiss and snarl.

*   *   *   *   *

housing

Now that you're Chairperson of the Housing Authority, Mr. Blandings, can you say a few words about the ideas you'd like to put into place? What would you like to see happen?

Well, first of all, I'd like to see more concierges. You know, people who will take care of those big buildings on the street. A great idea to have someone who lives right on the premises, who will keep the building in good repair, who'll help tenants with little problems that might arise, who will sweep the sidewalk, hold a key for you or deliver a message, hang out around the door, watch out for strangers and dangers, who will be the organizer, greeter, housekeeper, floor manager. sparkplug, maître d'....

In other words, you think that concierges will keep up property values, lower long-term maintenance costs, and raise the spirits in the building too, is that it?

Right, and I want to see them smoking Gauloises, and wearing berets, and bringing home those long loaves from the boulangerie on bicycles — we need more quaintness in city life, you know what I mean?

I think I do. What else do you have in mind?

Well, let's put apartments in some of those office buildings. Look at them — open for business eight hours a day, dead space for 16, while the housing market is tight as a drum. Let's find some people who want to live right in those buildings, right in the offices themselves. I mean, we'll put the office furniture on casters. We'll bring in Murphy beds, footlockers, things like that. They'll have jobs during the day, so they'll be out of there, or better yet maybe they'll work in the same place.

Look how this would also help our transportation problem. Look at the savings on security costs and answering services. Plus flexible working hours, since the offices could be open evenings. Also, let's have these offices put in homey touches, refrigerators and stoves, or fireplaces for example. Think of how it would loosen people up to have staff meetings around the hearth while it's snowing outside....

Now flip the situation around. Look at all those private houses which are locked up all day. What a waste! You may not realize these houses get *lonely* just sitting there, hour after hour. Let's encourage daytime occupancy, like bringing in musicians looking for a place to practice, for example, or people working the night shift, or people needing a quiet place to study or work at home. Let's have them use some of this bedroom-community space, fight crime, make money, and keep the block pumped up during the day.

You see, we need to inventory all the indoor space we have, and then find as many uses for it as we can. This is what we call the principle of multiple use. I want to see youth hostels in the public schools, a community center in the library, the homeless sleeping in city hall. And when a space is vacated, we'll re-use it adaptively. Take that former convent over there — an ideal residence for the retarded. I want to put a halfway house in that abandoned motel, elderly housing in that gutted-out warehouse....

But there are limits to this concept, aren't there? I mean, for the sake of argument, you can't have people sleeping on top of conveyor belts, can you?

Maybe not, though why can't factories be jointly occupied?

Look, you take a concept and push it as far as it can go, right? But I see, suppose you want to talk about people who are more exclusive, who want places just for themselves. That's perfectly okay. Here, we're going to use the principle of shared common space. Follow along with me and you'll see what I mean:

Come on inside this apartment building. You can see it's designed with common space in mind — most of the first floor is common space, in fact, which cuts down on burglaries. The concierge lives on this floor, of course rent-free. Look at this lobby with stuffed chairs and magazines, and good lighting for a change, where people are actually sitting and talking. Down the hall there's a little library, a meeting room, a game room, and a rumpus room for raising rumpuses, which we think is necessary given current social conditions.

In the basement, there's a laundry parlor, a sauna, a Nautilus room, a television lounge, a snack bar, a grocery corner, and a couple of rooms for strangers. We also have agency and business services coming right into the building on a rotating basis. Some tenants tell me they have all the things you'd expect to find on a cruise ship, which is actually how we designed it, for the way we think, why shouldn't life be a bracing voyage?

Now in the high-rises, we have common space on every fifth floor, social and recreational areas, classrooms, the same general thing. You can see that any building I have a stake in will place a premium on common facilities. The apartment building, not just the apartment, is home.

Before we leave, here's what the folks call Rogues Gallery. What happened is that everyone moved in here pretty much at once, and at the beginning nobody knew who their neighbors were. So one person thought of putting her photograph right above her mailbox, so that others could associate the name with the face. The idea caught on, because in recognition there is security. Soon everybody was doing the same thing; now we've got family shots, beefcake, and modeling stills. Anyhow, it was a real social stimulator, and in an offhanded way it turned out to be a crime deterrent too.

Okay, let's take a look at those houses over there. Small plots, right? They were originally designed bigger, but the owners wanted still more backyard space than we gave them. They got along pretty well, so they I think doubled their usable space by giving up some of their original yards and declaring them in common. Robert Frost says good fences make good neighbors. I say no fences make better neighbors, when you build up some trust and are ready for it. They still respect each other's privacy, maybe even more so, but there's an easiness, a less isolated feeling, that comes with fewer boundary lines. Look how they've planted fruit trees and made a grove right in the middle.

Most of the houses are fairly small on the inside, too. Money is tight. But one of them has a little more space than the others, and keeps up a room that all the people on the street can use for guests. Everyone chips in a little bit for upkeep.

I hear they also go over there just to lie down. Generally speaking, dropping in is encouraged, part of the local custom. People know what the limits are. But when you feel free to spend time in your neighbor's kitchen, or wherever, your own space becomes extended. Your square footage increases, so to speak...

Sir, these are all interesting and strange ideas, but with all due respect it seems to me that you're just circling around the real problem. We all know that most people still want homes of their own, but that fewer and fewer can afford to buy. Most people are priced out of the market. What are you going to do about them?

That's a good question. We answer it with the principle of diversified options. You've probably heard of creative financing — it's the same kind of thing here, except we're talking about creative occupancy. We're going to establish a mix that increases the number of housing options available, at a lower average price. Maybe this increases the average density a little, but again we make this up by the use of shared space.

What do you mean, exactly?

Well, to make houses move, the real estate people are going to promote joint ownership for unrelated individuals. Say these two singles want a home, but neither can afford one separately. So we encourage joint title, joint possession, joint payments. Let them each own half of a two-family, or a third of a three-family, as they like. Or we'll show them how they can remodel one house to get two master bedrooms, if they want to. Or we'll put the dual-master concept into new construction in the first place.

We'll use the latest in modular home design, to maximize options at minimum cost. We'll raise the mobile home to an art form. We'll have people live in leakproof domes, or yurts, or in pup tents in the forest on the edge of the city. We'll give out resident camping permits, so that people can stay semi-permanently in the woods, while we provide the hookups. We'll change the zoning laws to raise the maximum occupancy for traditional single-family houses.

We'll offer a little tax break for adding mother-in-law apartments and for dividing big old houses in general. We'll positively promote group houses, groups of unrelated people living together. There are as many arrangements like this as pebbles in the stream, and that's all well and good, because it keeps the options up, keeps costs down, and adds breadth and vigor to community life.

...By the way, if you want to live in a group house, you can drop down to the group house clearinghouse, which is one of the few places around that keeps group résumés on file. They also have a list of accredited house-sitters, with references.

We'll deliver our share of congregate housing for the elderly. But basically, we're going to encourage cooperative living across the generations, not just for one age group alone. That way, each age group will give to and learn from the other. We'll also be spending less for home repair, maybe for other elder services too, since the younger folks will be able to step in when the elderly can't handle things themselves. But the older people will be giving as well — cooking, child care, light cleaning, but especially personal support, wisdom, tradition, and linkage with the past.

Now in apartment buildings, we'll stimulate cooperative ownership, where the residents own the whole building, not just their living quarters. We want them to share in running the whole operation, and to think up novel arrangements and solutions for themselves. So we'll see to it that each cooperative building has a residents association. And that the associations themselves are federated. We'll make sure every association has officers, charters, committees, and that they're tough and participatory. We'll make a point of giving them technical assistance and training so that they know how to manage a building, and also how to hire a manager and hand out tasks. For housing projects, all of this goes double.

As for other tenant groups, we'll help them publish a landlord yearbook, with profiles of landlords in town, tenant satisfaction reports, lawsuit incidence, ratings on price, responsiveness, availability, maintenance, and other things a tenant needs to know, plus a digest of tenant rights....

But look, Mr. Blandings, let's face it, you're talking about the gentry, or at least the remnants of the middle class who are still going to be able to fit into decent housing one way or another. What about people who don't have the money, even if they're not desperately poor? What are they going to do? You've already got a long waiting list for subsidized housing, and it doesn't look like there's going to be a whole lot more.

Let me tell you, when my grandfather first moved here, he lived for many years in a boarding house. You remember, the residents have their own rooms, and they usually take their meals together. Let's bring them back. You know, when we think of boarding houses now, we think of long days at the mills and a rough existence. But it doesn't have to be like that. The boarding house can be a source of fellowship and joy. Younger people still seek them out in the form of fraternities and sororities, just like we did, and even group houses are boarding houses of a kind. Also, the boarding house can be terrific for rehabilitating people who've lived in institutions — it's got independence under supervision, social support, and graded responsibility, all at minimal cost.

So I'm going to sweeten the pot and call up some of my old hotel school contacts to see if I can round up a few prospective boarding house managers, and maybe give these prospects a little training on how boarding houses can be profitable for the manager, as well as inexpensive and cheerful for the lodger. At the least, I can import some models from out of town, and maybe I can chase down a little seed money for a demonstration project, possibly calling it fraternity houses for the mature.

Now, if you're not up for a full-scale boarding house, you can take in single boarders. I was reading that in the 1920s something like half the single-family houses had boarders of one kind or another. If you're living in a big house and especially if your marriage breaks up or your spouse dies or your kids move out, it's pretty obvious that after a while boarders make a lot of sense.

Maybe you don't want to bother with cooking; so let people make their own eating arrangements, or better yet let them live in simple rooming houses scattered through town. While rooming houses are usually plain and no-frills, that's not a given. Those apartment hotels with permanent residents are pretty fancy items, but dressed-up rooming houses are really what they are.

Finally, if you are an elderly person who is left alone and there are no kids to move in on, the chances are fair you will want a companion to live with. This despite our abatement insurance. So another thing I plan on is setting up home-sharing programs and au pair arrangements and matching services especially though not exclusively for older people. Younger people have matching roommate services, right? So we need the same thing for older folks, genteel and refined for sure, taking into account their special needs.

For that matter, why couldn't we have a matching service for landlords and tenants in general, with interview rooms and so on, so that people can get to know each other better before deals are closed, and can celebrate over a drink, landlord buys of course...

*   *   *   *   *   *   *   *   *

The single-room occupancy hotel isn't much, but it's home for assorted citizens on the margin, and they are part of the community. So when the developer comes in wanting to go condo, the others on the street pick shabby over upscale and they fight.

*   *   *   *   *   *   *   *   *

You'll have to excuse me. I'm still wondering about the dollars to finance all of this.

Exactly. Naturally, we're going to stimulate private investment and joint private-public ventures and bill every neighborhood as an enterprise zone. But if the private dollars aren't there and we want something badly enough, we'll go after it ourselves.

To start with, we're going to be mean and evil in collecting taxes from delinquent property owners, and we won't hesitate to foreclose when necessary.

We'll levy a surtax on absentee ownership; we'll pass a law that no property in the city can go unused for more than a certain length of time without fine, forfeiture, or public sale.

We'll penalize landlords who don't meet energy conservation standards, though we'll help out those who do.

We'll find some landowners who have a little land to give away, or who can donate it to our community land trust and write it off as a tax deduction.

We'll crack the whip on institutions and other tax-exempt organizations in the community to make an equivalent contribution in dollars or at least in services. If they won't cooperate, they'll find tax bills in the mail.

We're not necessarily in the market for housing, but once we get a property on our tax rolls, we're going to move it real fast. We'll put together our own organization to buy vacant houses and mortgage them to low-income residents at low interest rates. We'll sign up urban homesteaders. We'll put unemployed people to work fixing up abandoned housing and then we'll let them live in it cheap. We'll drown in sweat equity. We'll let out whole buildings for adoption, where groups of apartment dwellers can take over an entire property and fix it up and manage it themselves, and lease it with an option to buy.

We'll do whatever it takes. We'll lease property to the community development corporation. We'll print raffle tickets, or sell it at auction. We'll rent it free to nonprofits. We'll give it away. We'll burn it down if we have to and put up something else instead, but you can believe that housing is not going to just sit there.

I'm not finished. Now, we still have government grants and tax dollars coming in, don't we? Let's leverage each dollar for maximum impact. This means we need incentives:

For example, if 50 percent of the homeowners on a given street will agree to paint their houses or make other specified improvements, we'll match them bucket for bucket, or we'll give them a percentage rebate on the materials when they finish, or we'll agree to plant some trees. We'll furnish banners and other regalia for streets that are fixing themselves up so that they can be visible to the rest of the community and serve as models of inspiration and hope. Isn't this what government money is for?

We'll promote neighborhood pride and individual style by holding competitions for the most attractive restoration, the most original improvement, and so on, and give out prizes, just like entries in a state fair.

We'll encourage folks on a block to be foster parents to a vacant house or apartment, and help defray the costs of running it, so a needy family can move in.

We'll send around our town landscaper, our engineer, and all our other employees with building-related skills, and have them give consultation on an ability-to-pay basis, when it's asked for. We'll help set up home-related skills exchanges where they don't exist, especially for the elderly, and probably donate some time to them when they do.

We'll find people who know how to build houses and pair them together with people who don't. We may decide to raise our permit fees. But in exchange, we'll organize house-building and renovation and rent parties and pay for the beer.

We'll bring in staff from building trade companies into the neighborhoods to give self-help clinics and cost-cutting seminars.

We'll send people down to the construction sites on search-and-salvage missions.... Actually, for all of this we're going to focus on getting people to do these things themselves, because that lowers prices and is the best kind of leadership, just as Lao-tzu said.

* * * * * * * * *

A local citizen, you wouldn't call her rich, decides to repay her debt to her old neighborhood by starting a low-cost housing loan corporation. Greenline was its name. She raises $200,000 from her well-to-do friends and associates and one or two thrift institutions and puts it into a revolving loan fund. Neighborhood residents wanting to fix up their houses can apply for a housing loan at 60 percent of the going bank rate. The payoff is not in money returned but rather in money working locally. Neighborhood property values begin to increase, swelling neighborhood pride, fostering stability, attracting new business investment, and heralding an era of rebirth.

*   *   *   *   *   *   *   *   *

Well, I am impressed. But this sounds like a lot of work, even for a go-getter like you, Mr. Blandings. So my final question is how are you going to get all of this done?

Not by myself, I can tell you that. I'm going to create a space use panel of citizens to advise me on the use of all public spaces in town, inside and out. This panel will recommend best uses for any new property that comes into town hands. It will review all existing uses once a year and make suggestions for changes. It will encourage and process requests for public indoor space by town groups and individuals. All public spaceholders will be expected to justify and re-requisition their space yearly, and that will be on a competitive footing.

And when there's a case of new public construction or major remodeling, and for newly-acquired property too, we're going to have open bidding and also post prospective drawings and put them in the paper, so that the public can review and comment and perhaps even submit its own ideas. You can bet we'll listen. We're talking about public property, right? Public land is a public heritage, don't you agree? So isn't it true that the public should determine how it is used, and that therefore my job will become a whole lot easier? All it takes is a little vision....

*   *   *   *   *   *   *   *   *

Many Snowbirds were wealthy enough to leave their Florida apartments vacant three, six, even nine months of the year. Meanwhile, refugees living nearby....

*   *   *   *   *

urban design

Spokane, Washington: Horses stand peacefully near the city center. They belong to a carousel, which spins during daylight. It's a natural grazing place. Ride on the stallion: reach for the ring. Every city needs symbolism.

*   *   *

Downtown feels airy and open. It's quiet, since most traffic is routed outside. The quiet slows you down — it's harder to race. You feel as if you're walking through a pavilion, a campus, an extension of your living space, and that's what's intended. The street belongs to me; I feel at home here.

The walkways are built a little wider than usual to encourage street activity. Once, the sidewalks were linear speedways. Now there are planters, benches, flowers, kiosks, statuary, vendors, physical and psychic speed bumps. Three mph is all we want.

Every several blocks squares bring people together. They have fountains, gardens, fragrance, alcoves in the shade. Even the street furniture — the cushioned sofas, the contoured tables — makes people feel comfortable. The overall design helps people to relax and look around and make contact with each other.

*   *   *

The historical part of town is cobbled over. Residents work to make sure no turn is left unstoned.

* * *

One walker asks her partner, "Would you mind if I take a stretch?" She leaps for the exercise bars overhead.

A lifecourse winds in and out of the downtown area. Fifteen exercise stands, each with equipment stretching different muscles of the body. Each numbered, with pictographs and instructions, and charts listing skill levels by degree of competence. Morning and evening commuters pause at each station, as would subway trains.

* * *

Hawks and grey peregrines soar over town in spring and fall. They've changed their migration routes since the sanctuary was put in the town forest. Local topiary serves as beacon. Slower-paced members of lower-flying species use the rooftop bird feeders as rest stops.

The flower garden in the central square is arranged in a mandala. At other squares further on, the flowers trace out ancient symbols and proverbs.

A hydra-headed receptacle graces each street. One head for paper, another for glass, a third for metal. It took a while for the public to become more discriminating about its trash. They were unused to mythological solutions for urban problems.

* * *

The urban design takes into account basic human needs. That is why there are public rest rooms not far apart, and water fountains that work.

A while back, knowing there was no place to pee, some of the older men in town decided to take matters into their own hands and built a pissoir complete with sewage drains and held a public grand opening on the main street.

* * *

The narrow, tree-shaded streets save energy. The streets themselves have signs on each corner to tell you where you are, with address numbers on top to tell you where you are going. The numbers on the houses are large and luminous. That's what donations from the tree nursery and the foundry plus a little common courtesy can do.

The bus stops are sheltered, to protect against weather. In winter, radiant heaters inside the shelters keep you from freezing half to death if buses are running late. Colorful street maps, drawn by the neighborhood associations, are hung outside each shelter and also on street kiosks every half-mile or so. Handwritten notes on the maps tell the reader about the community as well as where he or she is within it. The kiosks double as neighborhood bulletin boards, and in warmer weather as refreshment stands.

·　　·　　·

In the North Country, the shopping area goes underground. Enclosed passageways substitute for open sidewalks, and floodlit grottoes for sunny squares. People live beneath the surface of life. One community talks of a rollaway roof over the shopping mall, while another wonders whether the cost of a giant dome would be paid back in new business activity and tourism.

·　　·　　·

The city planners have studied behavioral science; they know the effects of environment on psyche. They think of spirit as well as structure. They've organized a study group with architects and psychologists and pedestrians which meets monthly to make things better. They say, "Between us, we know about urban systems, social behavior, and feelings. Let's talk."

Every year the design competition is open to all. Entries which would improve the human environment are solicited. Scale models are constructed, and put on display. The public votes — balancing beauty, function, and cost in private ways. The winning entry is built.

Another study group meets weekly at a private home. They are utopians, planning a new town. They have joined together to buy land in the country. They work hard figuring out what their town will look like, what will go where. In a year or two, they may be ready to move the earth.

.   .   .

A street sign says

in a different color than the speed limit warnings. Most people thought the signs were a good idea, but some felt the noise traps further down the road were going too far.

.   .   .

The town buries its dead, those not wishing cremation, behind the town hall. This is still mostly true, though they're running out of room. Death is meant to be visible; how better can the dead live in memory? Their presence brings continuity with the past and the future.

At night, the cemetery is a trysting place. The wise old caretaker knows that burials and conceptions per year are roughly equal, which is about as it should be.

.   .   .

The woods part to reveal a shopping center. To get there, you leave your home and walk along forest trails, passing picnic groves and a pine-topped chapel. In some communities, home and commerce are woven into one. Here, there is material and spiritual separation. The woods allow for smooth transition, and gentle integration of the branches of your life.

.   .   .   .   .

health

The epidemiologists had trouble explaining why life expectancy in the community was five years higher than in the surrounding region. They thought: no hidden valley, no genetic isolation, no miracle diets. Finally, they said our evidence is not fully conclusive, but what we have points to (a) wellness, (b) prevention, and (c) self-care.

*   *   *

New clients take a wellness test at home and return it to the doctor's office. It's a 100-item, multiple-choice questionnaire about diet, sleep, exercise, friends, work, sex, stress, moods, history, symptoms, and general outlook on life, emphasizing changes over the past year. The client is also asked to mark on a 100-point scale how healthy he or she *feels*. The self-scored results yield a profile which helps the doctor in conducting the wellness examination.

The rationale behind the test is that high scorers feel better and live longer. This health care system doesn't want you to get sick. It says an ounce of prevention is worth a pound of cure. So most insurance plans entitle you to a wellness exam yearly, an office review, plus the growth therapy of your choice. They will give rebates for heart-lung fitness and appropriate weight. They'll cover you for the no-smoking clinic or the low-fat cooking class. (Such classes, now reimbursable, proliferate.)

During the examination itself, the doctor probes more deeply into areas covered by the questionnaire. Results are explained and interpreted, then discussed. Specific complaints get treatment, much as before. In addition, doctor and client together explore options for behavioral changes consistent with the client's own wellness goals. Jointly-agreed-upon prescriptions are made, and the client is encouraged to call the office monthly with further questions and follow-up reports.

Those goals are important. Each person taking the wellness test is also requested to write precise wellness goals down on paper and to enter them into a wellness contract with his health care provider. The goals are revealing, precisely the point. The contract defines responsibilities; it's signed and witnessed; it's subject to joint utilization review. This is health insurance in more ways than one. If you meet your goals, better health, at lower cost to you.

* * *

In reviewing its own goals one year, the Department of Public Health affirmed that it was committed to the health of the public, to the well-being of all the people, not only to the treatment of the sick. The next step was to put such a health care system into operation. This took commitment, and the cooperation of others, but mostly it consisted of a lot of little things:

.
.
.

At night, the hospital lobby looks like convention central. That's when most of the courses are given. Sign yourself up, or take in a show. The vitamin debate is about to begin. Can the yogi really stay under ten minutes? Readings from *Arrowsmith, Health* with Garner and Bacall. The operating room theatre is open, but looks like SRO once more.

The hospital also reserves Saturdays for kids, when health is marketed, pretty unabashedly. The health magician, the sugar blues band. For kids and the pediatric unit, it's a time and a half. For parents who can pull themselves away, it's a dropoff point and a breathing spell. For the hospital, it's education and public service, and not worth the price of admission.

Once a year is the kids' health fair, a counterpart of the adult version, when the hospital with other health groups co-sponsors health games, hands-on exhibits, stories, surprises, miracle cures, cartoons, stump the pharmacist, and make-it-yourself nutritious snacks from the 20-foot snack bar.

There are regular kid events too, kid-centered talks and discussions. After-school classes go on back-room tours, where they meet administrators and orderlies. They check in at the nurses station and talk with the patients. They get to know the terminally ill. They observe the E.R. from a respectful distance, and try out some of the new equipment, carefully. Season ticket sales are up.

* * *

" 'Most of my life has been spent in treating persons, one by one,' said Dr. Karl Menninger, the 83-year-old patriarch of the family. 'But as I become increasingly aware of the extent of misery and hopelessness in our society, I think more of preventing unnecessary suffering at the source, before individuals take or are forced down the wrong road.' "

* * *

The local medical society thinks: the well-baby clinic works out fine. But if that's what we value, why not services for well children, well teen-agers, well adults, and well seniors?

Personal letters go out. Not too much later, most doctors spend an afternoon a week at the wellness clinics scattered around town. They work out of church basements and community centers — whatever equipment is needed is stored in a closet and can be set up in ten minutes. People who are basically well come in for short consultations, averaging maybe five minutes each. It's mostly question and answer. If a longer time is needed, you can make an appointment at the office.

If you are sick, you can go to a sickness clinic, held in the same place at the same time on a different day of the week.

Or you can come to any of the screening clinics, on screening days. Rotating clinics at each community site, for blood pressure, heart, bowel, eye, sports, kidney, lung, an organ system of the month. Separate screening clinics for kids specialize in early detection.

Schedules are posted and publicized in each neighborhood. Monday — wellness clinic. Tuesday — sickness clinic. Wednesday — golf. Thursday — screening. Friday — anyone. Saturday — open house, mostly talk and demonstrations. Really sick? Call your doctor, go to another neighborhood, or come to the hospital.

* * *

The medical van parks by the projects, and, having gained consent, snatches people from the streets.

* * *

Next: A live call-in clinic, 24-hour staff on rotation. My kid was bitten by a dog. My dog was beaten by a kid. I've had these real bad headaches for the past three days. I think I threw my back out....

A seasoned and reassuring voice on the other end, able enough to dispense first aid and medical advice over the phone, and careful enough to tell each caller to get face-to-face attention if either of them has doubts.

One of today's calls is from the radio station. Would they consider going over the air?

* * *

Emergencies are separate. If you have one, call the medical emergency line, which is hooked up directly to the emergency room and is scanned by the ambulance service. They'll dispatch an ambulance instantly, or tell you what to do about burns or poison or shock, or do both. The same number, M-E-D-I-C-A-L, connects you to the right place all over the country.

The emergency room had become a 24-hour walk-in clinic anyway, so the hospital staff decided to institutionalize it. Instead of looking down on non-emergency cases, those people were in fact encouraged to drop by. There are two 24-hour rooms now. One (yellow door) is for pretty much anything under the sun, and is where you go as long as you can walk. The other (red door) is for full-blown, life-threatening emergencies only, no exceptions. Patients are expected to triage themselves.

* * *

Detroit: In the middle of the night, doctors are making house calls. If you need a doctor in the house, phone up, and someone will be en route within five minutes. The doctors on this service rotate over time slots, sort of an emergency group practice. Nurses prescreen the calls. The cost is prepaid via health insurance. Franchises are available in other cities.

Objection: Aren't home visits wasteful and unnecessary? Rebuttal: Personal care is never unnecessary. Ambulance calls could be much more wasteful.

Who wants to make house calls and be up all night? Interns and residents, as part of their training. Nurse practitioners, more and more. Retired practitioners, wanting to keep a hand in. Night owls. Doctors with lousy home life or two kids in college. Some who like to catch up on paperwork or read during dead time. And some who volunteer out of a spirit of service. They donate their time, as this is required for hospital staff membership.

*   *   *

On a country road, a cluster of people is standing by the bus stop near the general store. Bus pulls up. Driver gets out. "Who's first today?" The hollowed-out bus back is a clinic. The driver is an internist on clinic duty. The health bus hums along the highway, more or less on schedule, calling ahead when late. This bus likes free riders — people going to the hospital, motorists stranded in the snow, or teen-agers thumbing their way home from school.

The Happy Tooth Dental Van can fill you up on the spot. The Vetmobile tends to the local fauna.

When there's a shortage of doctors, and sometimes when there isn't, nurse practitioners take their place. The logic is that most complaints don't need a physician. The nurse practitioners know at least as much about treating minor illness and maintaining health as doctors, since that's the core of their education.

These two practitioners trained each other. Together they instructed R.N.'s. The R.N.'s rode with the paramedics. The paramedics counseled the EMT's. In teams they taught self-care to neighborhood groups. All of them joined in a health skills exchange. Gradually, they shaped a health care network that combined maximum diffusion of knowledge with least necessary degree of specialization, and that best served the people.

•   •   •

Self-care starts early in life. The fourth-grade class takes a full first aid unit and gets cards to prove it. Just about every kid knows how to treat a cut, ease a cramp, or help a person who's been seriously injured.

Courses on self-care are oversubscribed. (You can rate yourself before and after.) This is a change from the empty rooms when virtually the same courses were called hygiene.

Adult Care is published by the county health department, modelled after the successful infant version, the authors believing that adults need care too.

"If the first $500 or $1000 that families spend on health care each year came out of their own pockets, there would be a built-in incentive to limit trips to the doctor and to practice more self-care. The government could use the money saved by providing less-than-full insurance coverage to finance courses for consumers on basic health care, physical-fitness programs and public education campaigns against smoking, obesity and the other major lifestyle illnesses of modern society."

Washington State: The Department of Social and Health Services invests in prevention, puts together a 164-page book called *Healthy Choices* with health promotion tips and local resource information, and distributes 50,000 copies free all over the state and to interested outsiders and waits for the results to come in.

•   •   •

What makes referrals easier is a pocket-size directory of health care professionals in the area, listing all members by discipline, education, certifications, affiliations, office hours, usual fees, insurance procedures, MasterCard or VISA acceptability, handicapped accessibility, housecall availability, bedside manner, willingness to write generic prescriptions, and an optional paragraph's worth of self-description.

Photos were eliminated by close vote. However, next year's edition will try out consumer satisfaction ratings, based on evaluation forms turned in by patients after completion of treatment. They'll print up a few more copies. If successful, the plans are to spread the rating concept to other professions.

As an adjunct to the guide, you can call up the inter-hospital office and request a health care professional in the area you need. Family practitioners are a specialty. Not only will the office make at least two referrals, but it will send them to you in writing and also mail them to the persons referred to, with the request, if necessary, that you be seen as soon as possible.

*   *   *

Excelsior, Minnesota: Dr. Milton Seifert, a family practitioner, has an advisory board of patients. He provides the treatment. They set his fees, collect his debts, evaluate complaints, and regulate the non-medical aspects of his practice. Why not? Isn't the doctor supposed to be responsive to patient needs? As Dr. Seifert says, "...not only does the individual patient share responsibility for his medical care, but patients collectively share responsibility for the way health care is delivered."

*   *   *

The nurse's office, with its rack of tip sheets, is Wellness Exhibit #1. These used to be the health tape transcriptions until the self-care flow diagrams came along.

The pediatrician's waiting room is Wellness Exhibit #2. The Visible Boy and Girl, health testing equipment, health-related playthings, booklets, quizzes, posters, blown-up photographs, old-time instruments, changing exhibits from the historical collection.

The Medical Goodwill Center is Wellness Exhibit #3. They'll take sign-ups for organ donations, and hand out literature for your friends. If you're healthy, they'll go for your marrow and sperm. Plenty of people need someone to talk to. Gifts of time are always accepted. Perhaps you also wouldn't mind driving someone home.

*   *   *

Coin-operated games in the shopping mall. Drop in two quarters, strap yourself tight, watch the lights flash, and listen to your body. Play inner space invaders. Measure your resting metabolic level. Jump up and down for a minute, and test your response to stress. How's your white cell count today? Wouldn't you like to check your iron? See if you can change those beta waves into alphas. A health game store is opening up soon, "a total health care experience."

•   •   •

Mom slept in the hospital room when Johnny had his operation. Parents and spouses often sleep in. The hospital encourages it, says it's good for recovery, also lowers nursing costs and hence the bill.

Blue Shield gives rebates to maternity patients going home a day or two earlier.

On the maternity ward, volunteers of a certain age come in simply to hold the infants between feeding and changing times. Babies start out in life with unconditional affection, unconditionally given.

The hospital warmline calls when the patient gets home. How are things going? How did you find your hospital stay? If you like, we can come and visit. Give us a ring if we can help; or if you want, we'll call again. The warmline volunteers handle much of the service evaluation, advocacy, and follow-up care.

•   •   •

The Hypertension Club meets and munches no-salt popcorn and talks about high and low stress points of the week. Like weight watchers, they squeeze in weekly, and reward or castigate themselves depending on their systolic/diastolic counts. They have a teacher, or "coach," who comes over from the local medical center once a month to give them advice and cheer them on. They've bought a sphygmomanometer with digital readout, and they take turns using it at home and lowering their pressure by will.

*   *   *

The Pharmacognosy Club harvests medicinal herbs.

*   *   *

The guest speaker on hospices got the church group interested enough to start its own. Members read the literature and got the professional backup. Theirs wasn't a textbook hospice, physically — it was basically a tax-delinquent property the church hustled and renovated after Mass — but it won its affiliations with its open heart. Life could be left with boundless love.

Another group opened an Exit House, where people who were usually (though not always) terminally ill carried out their own departures. Clients drew up their own death plans and arranged the appropriate ceremonies. Most would meet first with the exit counselor, the angel of death.

The Birth House lies across the street from the hospital. A cozy bedroom instead of a hospital bed. Calico instead of white muslin. A warm and comfortable place for a Birth Day, for bringing forth a new person into the world.

The midwife is making her third house call of the day and swears that the obstetrician is going to handle the next one herself. Why are so many people having their kids at home?

*   *   *

The local medical society has evolved into a larger association, composed of any health care professional wishing to join. Acupuncturists through X-ray technicians have all learned to work cooperatively with each other. Contact is also kept up with folk healers who do not fall within traditional or even non-traditional health care boundaries. Everyone's work is supported insofar as it proceeds according to shared health care principles. The doctors may feel superior inside, but that's not the point. The focus is on respecting and utilizing what others can do, not what they can't.

Many of the health care professionals in the area have formed their own health maintenance organization. Their HMO sells stock: it's publicly owned. Because it is more accountable and more passionate than its larger competitors, it tends to offer more service for less money.

In any case, the community attracts professionals who believe in integrating holistic and traditional and sociocultural approaches to health. All these caregivers are paying more careful attention to each other's work. The disciplinary lines are blurrier. The inservice meetings are livelier. The referral network is broader and tighter. More healing energy is directed outward — a citizen's advisory committee makes sure of that. Another task force is updating and enlarging the Hippocratic oath.

* * *

Wellness scores have gone up during the last few years, while the birth-adjusted death rate has dropped. The community was all-but-offered a grant to find out why, but almost said no, thinking it already knew. Then it reasoned it could divert some money to design a training program and write a training manual that other communities could use to teach their own residents nationwide.

So now researchers have arrived to probe the causes and to prolong life. We wish them well. But for now the assumption is that wellness works, that prevention works, that self-care works, and the health care resources of the community have been organized to deliver services accordingly.

* * * * *

*

*   *   *

*

Las Vegas Night at the Visiting Nurses Association. The public sector's response to the New Federalism. You have to raise money somehow.

Spin the wheel as you come in the door. Take a chance on a double bypass. Beat the odds and play Risk Factor. Think of life as points the hard way.

Those nurses can sure put on a revue. Give some blood before you leave.

*

*   *   *

*

safety

The bugle call early Sunday morning signals the weekly meeting and drill of the town militia. "A well regulated Militia, being necessary to the security of a free State...."

• • •

In a time of particular hardship, and after heated internal debate, one community builds a four-gated wall around itself and maintains volunteer security guards with badges and uniforms and radios and nightsticks at checkpoints so that neither strangers nor anyone else can get in without a photo ID issued by the Police Department.

• • •

The people in another corner of the kingdom, having already banned guns, decide to remove the locks from their houses.

They reason that the lock industry is the only industry that preys exclusively on human vice — that even firearms can be used to hunt food. They figure that short of a world-class security system anyone wanting to enter their homes could do so, and that an open door deters more than a simple lock. They argue that someone has to make the first and if necessary unilateral move toward proper public morality. They engage in public education on Fourth Amendment rights. Without advertisement or ado, they stop locking up and see what happens.

The locks come off around the schools too. The superintendent says that if the kids want to hang around the cafeteria or shoot baskets at 3:00 a.m., that's what liberty is all about. Hey, it's their school, their parents' tax dollars, and education means freedom as well as responsibility.

* * *

The electric company goes to school and rigs a little class demonstration. Here are some loose wires — anybody want to come up and touch them? Now what might happen if they brushed together and there was this curtain nearby?

The gas company warns about gas leaks and leads the children through a sniff test. The fire marshal talks about home fire drills and escapes. The doll figures in the model house have finally learned to avoid accidents. The kids come home with more literature than their parents want to read.

The utilities print safety messages on their envelopes. They send safety stickers with their bills, for the stove, the oil burner, the hot water heater. The Red Cross distributes packets of skulls-and-crossbones, concentrating on parents of newborns. The skull and crossbones is one of the first symbols a child learns.

* * *

The Driver Ed car buzzes till its belts are snapped. Here's one of the toughest courses in school, with points off for looking at the instructor the wrong way, or in fact when you're driving for looking at the instructor at all. Only Driver Ed graduates have a 50-50 chance of passing the road test the first time. Only Driver Ed graduates can be recertified every four years instead of two. Mostly Driver Ed graduates win the annual safe driving rally at the speedway. Plus insurance breaks (more for honors graduates), and a discount at some dealers.

More than one moving violation in any 12 months costs you the price and time of a driver re-education course, tougher than the original, over and above ticket fines. No-shows have their licenses revoked.

* * *

The Police Department offers a community course on how to prevent home burglaries. They are high on block watches. They demonstrate equipment options in the crime studio, and make specific model recommendations for different budgets. The last class meets in the lieutenant's house while the sergeants try to break in.

Another course in unarmed self-defense is even more popular. The curriculum includes basic preventive strategies, verbal techniques with class role-plays, tricky gambits and their limits, personal meditations and centering exercises, martial arts training (usually held outside so that spectators can watch), and debates between advocates of passive vs. active resistance.

.   .   .

The merchants association has a Safe Haven program, a resting place for anybody needing one — a child harassed coming home from school, a victim of a street attack, someone who is confused, or lost, or sick, or who needs momentary shelter.

One store on each block shows a Safe Haven decal, conspicuous by its presence. Inside, there's a place to sit, a back room to lie down in, a cup of coffee, a nearby phone, some comforting words, and a good sense of what further help might be needed and who might provide it.

.   .   .

Kids at school learn street manners from Officer Friendly. Kids at home have latchkey buddies to call.

.   .   .

Some companies get together and pool their security guard patrols, spread them out in a zone defense and get at least the same amount of coverage for usually less money.

These security guards learn the human relations business. They get exercises in listening, in empathic communication, and recall. And they learn other useful things they can do while on duty — minor maintenance, light filing, returning phone calls, studying criminology, watching out for safety violations. Some security guards double as auxiliary police, talk with kids on the block, keep an eye on the street.

* * *

Madison, Wisconsin, news item: In an effort to prevent street crime, the city votes to set aside funds to subsidize cab fares for women returning home late at night.

* * *

Every Saturday morning, for years now, the anti-nuclear group holds a vigil in the plaza. They just stand. The police chief takes a turn now and then, as a witness of his own concern. The civil defense officer, though, is a regular member. His job includes planning for nuclear disaster, but he knows what bombs can do, and to him antiwar and civil defense and public safety are one.

* * * * *

NUCLEAR WAR
NO SHELTER-NO ESCAPE

WARNING

The Board of Health of Boston
has determined that no occupants of this building
will survive a nuclear attack.

NUCLEAR WAR
has no cure. It can only be
prevented.

fire

The job of the fire prevention chief is to put out fires before they start. She can smell an oily rag at a hundred yards. She spars with the contractors and the home remodeling people, ensures that energy conservation is fireproof, takes a special interest in abandoned buildings and warehouses, answers citizen questions over the phone, handles most of the guest appearances, gets her sections into the housing code, and is ruthless in tracking down violators.

• • •

The chief also coordinates the annual inspection program, with her sharp-nosed crew. Each household in the community gets a home visit. A fire prevention officer, with prominent ID offers a free fire safety inspection; right now is okay, or later on by appointment. If the offer is accepted, he tours the house with the householder, marking down any questionable or hazardous areas. When was your chimney cleaned last? Smoke detectors? Extinguishers? Alternate exits? Fire drills? Code violations are noted in red.

The householder gets free prevention literature, a copy of the no-carbon inspection form, and detailed instructions on how to eliminate cited hazards. The secretary at the station makes most of the follow-up calls. Over the course of a year, the officers get around to every house; they'll return next year with last year's form.

In the calculus of freedom and coercion, the home inspection program right now is voluntary. (Not for public buildings, though.) True, the banks and insurance companies which receive the results sometimes feel a little differently. But the community says that insofar as possible social contingency management should rest on incentive, not force. So safe houses get a door sticker, and their occupants a letter of thanks. If inspection is declined, the officer hands out a checklist and his business card; the offer is always open, and if there are any questions he'd be happy to help.

The community believes fire prevention saves lives and money. It believes in prevention so strongly that it acts on its belief, and allocates a third of its yearly fire budget for prevention activities. Then it studies fire rates, especially in inspected vs. non-inspected homes, equating for extraneous variables.

·   ·   ·

The town buys smoke detectors and extinguishers and places them in every public building and public housing unit. For all homes, a beeping detector and a charged-up extinguisher each get you a $5 credit off your local income tax.

The fire fighters watch out for large luminous stickers in the windows: red for small children, red with a yellow stripe for older or handicapped people who might need special help to escape, animal stickers for dogs and cats.

An engraved notice on the handle tells you that it costs an automatic $1000 to ring a false fire alarm.

·   ·   ·

The paid fire fighters recruit and train volunteers. They have quotas, each one reach and teach one. The volunteers are auxiliaries, like auxiliary policemen, who wear fire fighters' hats and have assigned responsibilities.

The auxiliaries also take on specific tasks in their own neighborhoods. They organize checks of the alarms and hydrants and fire zone markings. They coordinate the red sticker program. They organize block watches in high-arson areas. They post the reward notices. They are known by the absentee landlords, and trusted by the insurance companies. They sell tickets to the ball. They assist the fire prevention officer in home consultations and follow-ups and sometimes do the inspections themselves. They train a fire warden for each block. Each block, each house ideally, is to be a fire prevention station.

*   *   *

Many fire fighters in Hispanic neighborhoods take the conversational Spanish course offered free. All of them carry a laminated Spanish Fire Card, with two dozen phrases for emergency use. ¡Salga Afuera! ¡Por Aquí! ¿Hay Alguien Adentro? ¡No Entres! These come in handy every so often, and they have saved a few lives.

*   *   *

As part of the town giving program, you can adopt a fire truck. (The town is turning itself into an adoption agency.) Adoption here means washing and waxing rights, and affixing the decal of your choice. For $X more, you can slide down the pole. For a little extra, they'll turn on the siren for you.

In a move toward greater efficiency, the Fire Department buys smaller trucks to fight smaller fires.

*   *   *

While waiting at the station for calls, the fire fighters read great books, give CPR classes, collect toys for the needy, go out on ambulance calls, train for other careers, mail bills for services rendered (high-rises cost extra), handle the cash register across the street while the owner is out for lunch, play croquet with the kids on the lawn, hold visiting hours for climbing over the engines, have open houses on fire safety, engage in political debate, show instructional films, review the disaster plan, practice for the muster, arm-wrestle the off-duty police, and teach the junior fire fighters' course.

And when not on assignment, they cook; then they sell their stuff right out on the patio. That's one of the reasons the fire station has become a snack bar as well as social center. They also market their goods under contract with a local packager who sells them to local groceries under the Firehouse label. Fish chowder a specialty.

•   •   •

This fire fighter walks a beat. He's a cop. Or actually a "safety officer," since police and fire merged. "Fire fighters" carry guns and make arrests. "Police" cruisers stow hoses. Safety officers expand their vistas. It's that or layoff.

•   •   •   •   •

emergencies

Sharp rings wake the rescue squad. Possible stroke in the next village over. Into the van, on the road, cruise at 80, there in seven minutes. A stroke all right, the victim flat but breathing. Easy with the stretcher. Ten more minutes to the hospital.

The driver and crew are volunteers, college kids, EMT's. It's rural out there. No rescue squad in their neck of the woods, so they become one. No formal credit, though they usually get free health care anywhere in town. They rotate shifts, sleep in a special dorm. It's tough work, which is not to say they like it, but it's essential.

* * *

Still in the country: The ambulance sits in someone's driveway, while the ambulance driver of the day putters around the house, wearing a beeper. The backup ambulance, meanwhile, is parked in front of the funeral home. It's a hearse, which converts quickly to an ambulance when its equipment package is shoved in. The vehicle does double duty, is an instrument of life and death.

* * *

An adhesive sticker stays glued to each telephone receiver. It has police, fire, and ambulance numbers in luminous lettering. Bright-bordered, hole-punched cards with 24-hour services hang from the walls: poison center, crisis hotline, state police, local hospital. The same numbers are in 32-point type on the back cover of all phone directories.

The service club brings stickers and cards to all new residents. It also distributes emergency first aid booklets, courtesy of Red and Blue Crosses, with small ring binders that go right by the phone. The town mails revisions with its tax bills, extras for landlords, figuring that crisis knowledge will some time save lives. Even if not, the town still thinks of its moral obligation.

*　　*　　*

In a true emergency of any kind, call 911. It's a national number, for all communities, free from a pay phone, backing up any seven-digit numbers now in use. The operator steers calls to police, fire, ambulance, whatever else is tied in. Children practice calling in school. The elderly get one-button wrist units, with remote control.

911 is only for life or death. Okay, now let's see how far we can discriminate. 811 will be for serious problems. 711 will stand for minor complaints. How many gradations can people master? We'll keep all the -11 numbers free and aim eventually for 1-10 scaling.

*　　*　　*

A tornado is heading this way. A horn blasts twice through the town. The weather station calls the phone company. All the phones in the area start to ring, whether busy or not. It's a phone override system, designed to warn people of possible disaster.

*　　*　　*

Breakdown on the highway. Use your road map to get assistance. On maps put out by the state and by major oil companies, there's a red-and-white reflecting HELP panel that you can place in your window or flash along the road to motorists passing by.

*　　*　　*

People in town will tell you they're survivalists — that is, they want to survive. Most keep a two-week supply of food and water in their basements or somewhere else nearby. They don't feel superior for having it. They know they may never have to use it. They neither court nor expect disaster, but it's cheap insurance. They know that if disaster strikes, and some survive, they will have an edge; and also that if most people have edges, the social compact will be more likely to hold. In any case, it will be a lot easier for the community to get back on its feet if the necessities of life are temporarily provided for.

Utah: Survival condos are for sale in the far country. Built into the earth, designed to withstand all but the closest hits. Windows with painted views of mountains or prairies, owner's choice. Six months' provisions. Common space for indoor recreation and get-togethers.

The survivalists go hunting. The family that preys together stays together.

And twice a year the people drill. En masse. They know what to do if disaster strikes, and where to go. They grumble, crack bitter jokes, move at three-quarters speed. But still they heed the Emergency Planning Office motto, "To fail to plan is to plan to fail," and opt for the extra margin of safety.

*   *   *

Susie has 101 degrees this morning, and there's a big meeting at work I have to get to. I phone up Sitters on Call. They'll send someone over, even at the last minute, who knows how to care for a sick child. S/he might bring over the get-well satchel, or take Susie to the doctor if really necessary. I'll leave a number where I can be reached, and I'll be in touch later on.

If you have an emergency, but not a life-threatening or medical emergency, then call up the Mutual Aid Network 24 hours a day. (In another town, it's FISH.) They have volunteers on call who will provide transportation, run an errand, cook a meal, hear you out, hold your hand, say something kind, argue your case, and do all the things that neighbors are supposed to do for each other.

*   *   *

Arlington, Mass.: The town's Instant Committee (a flying fish) of general-purpose people will when called upon mobilize themselves to help any cause, on any occasion. They are giving doing good a good name.

*   *   *   *   *

transportation

Transcript of the testimony entitled "Report and Recommendations of the Transportation Advisory Committee to the Planning Department and the Public at Large":

1. Citizens and Department members: Having conducted considerable research and having surveyed public sentiment in depth, our major conclusion and recommendation is that it's best for people to walk.

Now that more people are working closer to home, or in the home itself, walking is more feasible. Walking also offers advantages not duplicated by other transportation systems:

• It is immediately available. Departures may take place at any hour of the day, with no waiting.

• It requires little special equipment which might get lost or damaged. Maintenance costs are minimal.

• It is infinitely flexible, able to cover a limitless number of individualized routes, and able to navigate terrain as well as or even better than most four-wheel-drive vehicles.

• It promotes energy conservation, by using renewable resources.

• It is free.

• It is sociable, for neighbors are seen en route, and walkers are inclined to wave hello or stop and talk for a moment.

• It exercises the whole body, especially the cardiovascular system. (Those in a real hurry can jog.)

• It is centering, conducive to personal affirmation, and receptive to stock-taking before the day, mind-clearing in the middle, and decompressing when the work day is done.

• Perhaps most important, it encourages the walker to enjoy the journey along the way, to arrive unrushed, unhurried, and in a state of grace.

• • •

2. When people can't walk, have them ride bikes. Set up a bikeway stretching from one end of town to the other. A separate pathway, not just a strip of street where cyclists will get squashed into the curb by thoughtless drivers and other yo-yos.

• Join with other towns to extend the bikeway through their land so that it can be used for medium-distance commuting. Put up traffic signals and crosswalks that cyclists must observe for pedestrian safety.

• Keep abreast of bicycle technology, especially the latest lie-down designs, allowing the prone cyclist to gain more efficiency and speed and ride for longer distances.

• Put bike carriers on buses to make portages easier.

• For local hops, have the town buy a fleet of one-speeds. Paint them canary yellow, engrave them with noneradicable numbers, and park them at bike racks every block or two. Anyone wanting to go anywhere in town can then pick up a bike, pedal it away, and drop it off at the nearest stand.

• Put bike helmets alongside the bike racks, and child seats you can slide on. Cover the racks to guard against the elements. (Bikes needing maintenance can be parked in special slots and appropriately tagged.)

• Think about putting bicycle lanes along every main road, in addition to the bikeway, and study why these lanes sometimes don't work.

• Step up production of bicycles built for two.

• Encourage bicycle taxis to roam the streets.

• Check the feasibility of a bicycle bus.

- Outfit bikes with carrying containers and use them for local deliveries.
- Give them to postal workers for delivering the mail.
- Give them to messengers for handling small parcels. Contact United Parcel Service and ask about subcontracting.
- Use heavy-duty bikes like small pickup trucks. Put motors on them when you have to.
- Reserve some low-slung tricycles for small children, and adult-size tricycles for the elderly, and unicycles for hot dogs.
- Require the teaching of bike safety in the schools.
- License all private bikes to raise consciousness and pick up a few bucks. Keep road tests as an open option.
- Hold bike rodeos and skill and daredevil competitions and jamborees.
- Ask the bike shops to give courses in bike repair so that people can fix their own, especially on the road. Design repair kits riders can put in saddle pouches. Hang a few on the bicycle lanes.
- Put a couple of cops on bicycles and have them cycle a beat.
- And put them on motor scooters to patrol the bikeways and bike lanes and have them carry emergency equipment for helping the disabled.

Figure that for each bus or rail coach you can buy 100 bicycles, maybe more. Then factor in maintenance costs, ridership patterns, health benefits, and the most cost-effective option is obvious. Of course, with less bus and auto traffic, bike riding will be that much safer too.

Also, don't stop at bicycles. If people are into roller skating, set up skating lanes. Put a parallel strip beside the bikeway for joggers. Since we get snow, change some bike paths to ski trails in winter. Mark off best routes on the frozen ponds. Place a small ski tow on the big hill and have folks slalom down. Train some Saint Bernards with flagons, or at least mutts with cocoa. Dogsleds?...

• • •

3. While our recommendations stress walking and biking, we will still want fuel-powered mass transit, especially for trips of a few miles or more. Therefore:
- Buy double-decker buses for efficiency and style.

- Redesign the buses. Make their interiors fit for people, not zombies. Begin by facing the seats toward each other so people can talk.
- Encourage people to get up and move around. Take out the seats altogether and have passengers sit on cushions or carpeted mounds, so long as safety is provided for.
- Experiment with indoor-outdoor carpeting on the floors.
- Hire an engineer to reduce the interior noise. Find a decorator to redo the interior decor.
- Put in some folding tables for people to work on, and overhead reading lamps.
- ...some tilt-back seats for taking naps.
- ...some hanging plants, as long as they don't obstruct the driver's view.
- ...some battery-powered vacuums on the wall so that passengers can take responsibility for their own environments.
- Make room for a small newspaper and magazine rack. Try out decks of cards and puzzle books and kids' activity kits.
- Build in a Mr. Coffee machine.
- Have smoking and non-smoking sections. Ask riders to fasten their seat belts.
- Place stereo earphones under each seat so that passengers can plug into music, sermons, language lessons, or news analysis.
- Stick a coin-operated microcomputer in the back, near the dollar-bill changer, and let people work on their personal finances.
- Put survey forms in the seat backs so that the transit authority can find out what riders want.
- Run trial routes in neighborhoods, based on petition.
- Hang up bulletin boards for notices. Make it policy to display public service ads for free. Hold a "Mr./Ms. Bus" contest and change the faces every month.
- Sponsor commuter puzzle contests, with weekly clues. Post the winning entries.
- Put thoughts for today on the outside of the buses. Switch them around every so often. We like Thoreau's "The swiftest traveller is he who goes afoot."
- Figure out what kinds of live entertainment, amateur probably, might fit into the ride. Recitals. Auditions. Folk tales.

Appoint an emcee. Post a schedule, or mark special buses as show buses. Take reservations.

• Follow the example of the big-city subways, where underground music is often the norm. We also need a good bus song, something like "Take the A Train" or "Clang, Clang, Clang Went the Trolley".... Be open to suggestions.

A humming noise in the bus, a low buzz. There's nothing wrong with the engine. What is it?...It's an om sound. People are chanting on their way to work.

Now, we believe that mass transit should cost the rider his or her fair share. The bus system in this case should at least break even. But most of the amenities we've recommended will have low to negligible cost, and these costs, like the amenities themselves, can be phased in over time.

Certainly, less motorized traffic will make for smoother driving, thus lowering fuel expenses. We should keep costs down as well by being quick to test new technologies. Engines, for example, which can run efficiently on our homemade fuel. Electrification, from our own generating plant.

Our Committee has also studied the possibility of a no-frills or steerage class, where everyone has to stand and some may have to hang outside, but we have decided against recommending that option at this time. However, one basic way to cut costs and therefore prices will be to form a bus drivers' cooperative. Those who want to and who can pass a stiff driver's exam can drive a bus for a day or so a month in exchange for fare reduction, while others can work on interior or exterior bus maintenance, whose importance should go without saying.

We can also keep the budget in balance by attending to the revenue side — with special ridership offers, with discounts for heavy users, with bounties for new recruits, with monthly to lifetime passes, with excursion fares, with contribution boxes, with off-peak reductions, with gift subscriptions, with a free-ride lottery, and particularly, if our legislators go along, with gas tax diversion.

But transportation strictly within the downtown area should be free. That's a necessary inducement to commerce and to city life.

Here we need a frequently-operating jitney bus following a tight circular route. Or maybe something a little flashier, like the open cars that take visitors around zoos.

• • •

4. Our emphasis on self-propelled and mass transit does not mean we reject private cars. Cars have their uses, and even if they didn't we surely haven't the power to abolish them. What we can and should do is to pair incentives for using more fuel-efficient forms of transportation with moderate and reasonable disincentives for private car travel. Here are some moves we can make on a local level:

• Impose a stiff graduated surtax on both new and used car purchases and be willing to test its legality.

• Tighten our local safety and inspection ordinances and tax for pollution according to the actual measured amount of emissions.

• Start voluntary carless Sundays and/or carless days of the week.

• Survey the potential acceptability of limited voluntary gas rationing.

• Trade in half the town's cars for motorcycles, but keep the old mileage allowances for those making the switch.

• Teach horns to say Arugah and other friendly sounds.

• Ban cars from downtown, at least from the main downtown shopping areas. Let them chase each other around a ring road. Naturally, if we extend our pedestrian mall, we will not have to ban cars as such, for there will be no place for them to go.

• Set up large parking lots around the periphery and have people take shuttle buses.

• Maintain a vigorous parking meter program. Keep fees high. Design the meters so fees double each hour without proof of purchase. Prohibit long-term parking and meter feeding during peak hours. Compensate by selling season passes. Hire enough ticket agents to hand out violation notices. Recruit minority youth on commission, and have them compete for prizes. Aim to catch 100 percent of violators, and post positive results.

• Enforce the violation notices, fiercely if necessary. Arrange to suspend licenses and triple costs if payment is not received within 24 hours. Slap superglued stickers, "I'm a Parking Violator," on the back bumpers. Buy a bunch of Denver boots painted with barracuda teeth and hunt down and immobilize any car whose owner doesn't pay up in time.

- (One town we contacted invests heavily in tow trucks, and keeps them cruising the main streets during the day. The drivers are trained to dress tough and act nasty. To them, parking violation is space rape. They take Polaroids for proof, and get bonuses for each car brought in, minus heavy fines for improper tows or damages...)

- Invest in a municipal loan fleet of electric microcars, like the bike pickup system we described before. As variations, charge an annual fee toward covering expenses; issue special licenses for using the cars, given only to people with good driving records and clean pasts; code the licenses magnetically and have them serve as ignition keys.

- Start media campaigns promoting the idea of neighbors buying a car together and using it cooperatively.

- Get on the taxicab companies to permit ride sharing to lower both fuel and personal costs.

- Bring in the commuter computer to set up car pools. Call C-A-R-P-O-O-L to arrange a match.

- Encourage large employers to buy vans and start vanpools. Encourage other drivers to start vanpools of their own.

- Let school buses pick up anyone, on a space-available basis.

- Let older people dial-a-ride when they need one. Link this effort with the FISH people, who will have a 24-hour vehicle on call.

- Egg on hitchhikers: Give each accredited hitchhiker a reflecting armband to wear or flash so that drivers will feel safer in picking up strangers. License long-distance riders if you have to.

- Revive the People's Free Wheels, sometimes known as Thumb Taxi. Those kids by the drive-in have nothing to do? Find them an old van, let them fix it up, and have the van roll up and down the avenue to be flagged by anyone needing a lift. If we can't get kids to drive the van, let's find parents who will do the job on rotation. Make this service free or donation-only. Maybe we can tap oil company windfall profits. Grungy will be okay. The appeal may be primarily to younger people, but the van should be available to everyone.

• If we can't find a van, maybe a hay wagon will do even better.

Please note that for much of what we've reported so far, *government may need to do very little.* Some of our ideas are operational right now. Most of what may be required is to keep track of what's already going on, to give gentle pushes to ideas already in the pipeline, to offer technical support, and to encourage private voluntary groups to do as much as they can...

Well, thank you very much. I'm sure we all appreciate...

Excuse me, we're not quite done. We have a few more ideas to put on the table:

• Try out cable cars for the romance, since we have the hills and especially if we didn't. Shouldn't public transportation be romantic?

• The town is on a river, right? So how about boats to get people from one place to another? Let's think about small boat ferries. Let's talk about paddling our own canoes. What about municipal motorboats, like Venetian vaporettos? Let's become the Venice of the Midwest, if that's where we are.

• Those hills back there cry out for an aerial tramway.

• Is there a non-demeaning way to establish rickshaw licenses?

• Give the police continuing education credits for taking courses in auto mechanics.

• Toss out the idea of a samaritan van, and let local businesses scramble to pick it up. The van will roam the town in bright company colors, and its personable driver-mechanic will stop to assist any motorist in trouble. No charge, but good publicity, and a fine public service. When they're not busy, maybe they can pick up a casual rider or two.

• We'll need a couple of special vans for the disabled — for medical transportation, for special pickups, for small grocery and drugstore deliveries.

• And while we're on vans, encourage social service agencies to buy some, possibly sharing the cost, so that agency staff can circuit-ride and deliver more services right in the neighborhoods.

Maybe this is a case where the town really ought to chip in, because our preferred approach is to bring services to the people rather than people to the services...

Thank you again. And now if we can...

• Find shopping carts to put near the bike racks. Baby strollers, too.

• Have the Public Works Department keep the sand boxes full in winter, especially on hilly streets. Build a small attachment to each box. Stick in some jumper cables, a scraper, a spray can of de-icer, St. Christopher medals, maybe a set of tire chains. If you borrow, you replace.

• Persuade the Turnpike Authority to put out coffee in heated alcoves next to the rest rooms beyond each toll plaza.

• Get private carriers to compete with each other for longer-distance trips. Promote executive coaches, with limited seating and reservations, bar service and hostesses. Show movies. Hand out macadamia nuts.

• Give high school equivalency courses at truck stops and over CB radios.

• Put the horse back on the highway. Consider that:

> The annual cost of operating a two-horse wagon and a four-ton truck is roughly the same... but the horse is quicker, does not pollute the atmosphere, and has a working life of 14 years — twice as long as the truck.

• Study stagecoach economics. Test-drive horse-drawn carriages. Even where the horse may not be cost-effective, think of the elegance involved.

• In Big Sky country, get shopkeepers to put up hitching posts.

• (One private pilot we know says if you can pool cars you can pool planes, and has a planepooling service about to take off at the local airport.)

• Finally, when visitors come to town, put self-service map racks at the entry points. Follow these up with foolproof directional signs, so that people don't get lost. Hire a few tourists to try them and report back.

• Phone booths go next to the map racks, with informational stickers on the phones. Make sure there's a no-nonsense traveler's aid society, with a nonrecorded voice on the other end. Visitors who ask should be able to find inexpensive or free private places for bed and breakfast, as well as news on community services and events.

I'm sorry, but we really have to...

You asked for our advice: here it is. What kind of transportation system do we want anyway? One that gets people where they are going quickly, but without stress or aggravation. One that is simple and flexible and maximally resistant to breakdown. One that relies minimally on fossil fuels. One that's non-polluting. One that does not require heavy capital investment. One that's cheap to run. One that enhances the options for both social contact and anonymity. One in which the journey itself is pleasant and refreshing. One which operates in a community which downplays the need for extensive travel in the first place.

We believe our recommendations meet these criteria. The next step is up to you. Accordingly, we move that you (a) approve our recommendations; (b) choose those responsible for implementing the different components; and (c) report back at the next meeting with sequential plans and time frames for each component action, to be followed by...

(Transcript of testimony ends here.)

•   •   •   •   •

*

    *   *   *

*

"So anyone who hopes to express the soul's interests through local community service is eventually disappointed. Two things become clear: first, the community cannot help us with our own feelings about getting older and eventually dying. And second, our work has been largely ineffective."

— Carol Bly

*

    *   *   *

*

church

The minister wonders: Why can't our church set up our own day care center for working parents, with our own staff, and have the parents put back some time into other church activities in return? We have the room downstairs, and the need, and a lot of retired people, and supposedly enough good will.

The parish committee asks: Why can't we find jobs or even make jobs for people in our parish who need them? It's not like we're without contacts and skills and the will to work.

The full congregation thinks: We are not only a center for the Spirit, but we are also a community center for those fortunate enough to belong. What else might we do to carry out God's will on earth?

*   *   *

The church develops:

...An internship program for seminarians, who take on small-scale community projects.

...A Pastoral Care Advocates program, where lay parishioners from several congregations are trained first to identify pastoral care needs (interpreted broadly) in their own churches, then to design and help implement programs to meet those needs.

...A community sanctuary, emergency food or housing for anyone who's hungry or needs a temporary place to stay. In the church itself, or in the homes of parishioners who have signed up.

...Nonsectarian meditations, for people on the way home from work.

...A policy of opening its doors to community agency programs, several of which are based right inside the church: the halfway house for alcoholics; the women's counseling center; the partial hospitalization program, for former inpatients; the veterans office, after the fire.

The church basement is an office complex, with bright-colored signs and a directory at the foot of the stairs. Tenants help out in fund-raisers, and earn income of their own. The copy shop co-op serves church and state, turns profits two ways.

*   *   *

On the bulletin board this week:

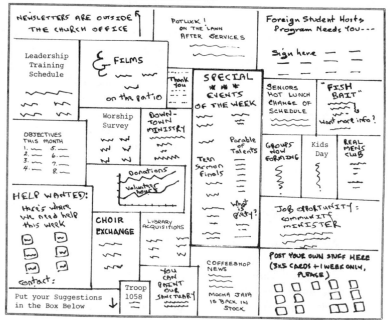

The ecumenical employment agency may land you a job through its computerized match-up service. The inter-church housing bureau has a 75 percent success rate in locating suitable living space.

*   *   *

Down on the range, cowboys rope dogies for glory of God. The church goes into the shepherding business, buys a ranch, makes money. Proceeds go to needy members, to the cowboy trainees, and toward capital improvements.

Others work in the church-owned canneries, hotels, auto repair shops, and so on down through the yellow pages. The church elders reflect: Why can't the church head full-tilt into the private sector and get rich?

The convent begins a media blitz in order to attract new nuns.

*   *   *

In the mall, there's a ministry for shoppers. The minister's office is near the family shoes, just off the meditation room. God and mammon are silent partners. A congregant comes into the office to ask "Why am I buying this?" and "What am I doing here?"

*   *   *   *   *

*

*   *   *

*

"We are living through the greatest crisis in the history of man; and this crisis is centered precisely in the country that has made a fetish out of action and has lost (or perhaps never had) the sense of contemplation."

— Thomas Merton

*

*   *   *

*

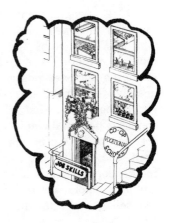

poverty

The neighborhood association goes door-to-door, asking its members what they think about sharing their income with the neighborhood poor. They talk about tithing. Well, maybe ten percent is not realistic, and five percent is shaky, but what about one percent? Is one percent asking too much? Can we do one percent right now? Can we have our own united fund?

Volunteer groups within the association arrange the collections and administer the funds. Some loans are made. Some cash-for-service transactions are consummated. Some money is set aside for emergencies. None of this is made to be a big deal, and it isn't actively promoted, but people come to know that the community will try to care for its own.

·　　·　　·

No money may mean no job. The association will help you look for a job if you need one, or point you to the right training program. It will grant small scholarships. It will also link you with the local co-ops and service exchanges, and show you where to get things done cheap or free.

·　　·　　·

Most people want to work. The welfare system (local minimum: income floor) is set up to make it easy to work for people who can. Job clubs for able recipients, mandatory after six months, are open to all. Clubs teach members to itemize their strengths and weaknesses, and to write down stepwise career goals. Members learn what jobs are available, what their requirements are, what salaries and promotions to expect, how to contact a potential employer, how to dress, how to speak, how to act, how to fill out an application, how to interview, how to get fired, and how to stay with what one has until something better comes along. There's a lot of role playing, videotape critiquing, mutual support, verbal reinforcement, reality testing, personal counseling, and active follow-up, plus a graduation ceremony and a cash bonus when a job is started and kept for 12 weeks.

The staff will also provide formal job training on a cost-sharing basis with local employers, with the recipient paying back a negotiated percentage following employment (discount for job clubbers). In a parallel program, staff train clients in budgeting, nutrition, consumerism, child development, and harmonious lifestyle.

*　　*　　*

Here's how you employ low-income (or retarded or handicapped) workers who have few job skills and are hard to place:

1. Find a clientele who matches your specifications and who wants to work.

2. Find a human services entrepreneur who will form a nonprofit Transitional Employment Corporation.

3. Get your clientele to sign up. They're in the Corporation now.

4. Recruit some companies who would be interested in hiring the workers you're about to train. (Conservative variation: take this step first.)

5. Have the TEC make a contract with the workers. The TEC agrees to hire, train, and pay them. The workers agree to do their best.

6. Have the TEC make a contract with the companies. The companies agree to employ the workers in their plants, and to

reimburse TEC on a worker-productivity basis, as well as for training expenses. TEC agrees to provide accountability, supervision, and support.

7. If the worker pans out, the company will exercise its option to hire and pay the worker on its own. Thanks to transitional employment.

*   *   *

The anti-poverty club runs barter programs for low-income people, helping them to get more mileage from their resources by trading them and spreading them around. Yes, it hopes to empower. First, it wants to teach (a) husbandry, and (b) trust.

A coalition of agencies and other groups serving the poor join forces in the Poor People's United Fund, raising dollars for services the patrician's fund will not support. Meanwhile, the Robin Hood Fund puts the squeeze on the Fortune 500.

*   *   *

More bills are accompanied by check-offs:

> *Check here* □ *if you'd like five percent of your remittance to go to a fund for those who can't afford to pay. We'll add our five percent if you do.*

More fees are starting to slide: when they don't, sometimes they can be waived altogether. Many museums, symphonies, athletic teams (then, institutions in general) fix their budgets so that a percentage of their services is free. These policies are publicized, though delicately. If you can't pay the full price, call in advance, or say so at the door, and pay what you can. More often than not, it works out. But sliding retail prices are another matter.

*   *   *

"Here the head of each household looks for what he needs, and takes what he wants without payment or obligation. Why should anything be refused him? There is enough of everything, and no fear that anyone will claim more than he needs."

*   *   *

The message of the group called Breakout is that money is sunshine and poverty dark, and that when you've had enough of the one you are ready to move on up to the other. The local community organizers agree that personal and economic empowerment are intertwined.

Not far away, though, the Simple Living Association turns down a few dollars by offering nonconsumer counseling to those who want or need to strip down their lifestyles.

* * *

The community believes that the taxing power of government should be used to promote social change. Therefore, the local tax structure is graduated and specifically designed to redistribute wealth.

* * * * *

agencies

The human services agencies, under the gun, commission an assessment of needs in order to respond better to the community. The major finding is that most people haven't a clue as to what agencies are around, much less what they do. If no one knows about the services, who can use them? And why should one care about the agencies, or give them support?

The agencies this time are jolted into action. They spend some dollars not to boost their image, but to build one; not to clean up their act, but to get one. Gradually, they move out of their fortifications and mix it up with the townies. This takes a while.

*   *   *

The agencies learn to tell their story to the public. They write snappy releases and cultivate the media. They pinpoint their mailing lists. They start suggestion systems, loose and formal. They institute complaint mechanisms. They conduct annual consumer surveys. They convene public hearings. They hold open houses, galas, fetes, with souvenirs, where people are tempted to walk in off the street and hear what's going on.

*   *   *

They recruit citizen boards. And they are *citizen* boards, made up of proletarians, not just big shots and power brokers. The makeup of the boards accurately reflects the makeup of the community, and more specifically of the clients served. Competition to join is stiff.

The agencies make a point of training board members. One staff person is responsible for keeping members advised and unjaded. The agencies want fresh-mouthed boards, and they have them. They want board members to give them a hard time, and they do. But the boards also go to bat when there are problems, like budget problems, and when their coalition of non-rich but well-connected voters bombards the legislature to spend more tax dollars on a particular social service, most legislators listen.

* * *

Each agency works to multiply its impact. It knows that there will never be enough human service workers, and that present staff must leverage their efforts as cleverly as possible. The more social hardships, the more service cutbacks, the more this is true. The agency faces a cruel paradox: the tougher the times, the greater the pressure to treat rather than educate. But the agency, with its rediscovered faith, recognizes that in the medium and long run the only way out is to help people help themselves.

The agency therefore invests in prevention — in preventing bad things from happening, in preventing bad from getting worse, and in engaging the help of the greatest possible numbers. Sharp criticisms arise from two opposite sides. One group argues that people need treatment now and that prevention is irresponsible. Another group says prevention is a sell-out, and that all-out *promotion* of desired personal and social characteristics is what's called for. The agency, acknowledging both criticisms, replies that the issue is not either-or but rather one of emphasis, the proper mix. The Board will be mixmaster. As for prevention, it's agreed to be fuzzy, hard to pin down and harder to evaluate. But the agency believes, crossing its fingers, that the payoff from prevention will not be exceeded.

* * *

And so agency staff are invited and invite themselves to talk to civic groups, schools, churches, workplaces. They'll talk anytime, anywhere. They spend time publicizing their availability, competing with bellygrams.

They educate through the media, acquiring a weekly column, a talk show. They become transit advertisers and cable masters. They start "Lifelines," a series of public service radio spots, and market them nationally. When someone says "access," they jump into place.

If an individual or group wants to start a new community project, or needs advice on a present one, agency staff are a phone call away. Consultation is key to the mission. They'll network, problem-solve, open a door. The Small Business Administration advises businesses. Community agencies advise the community, same principle.

*   *   *

Agencies shift skills according to the moment. They construe their mandate as flexible. When times are rough, they focus more on economic issues, since dollar pressures lead people to seek them out. They grasp the links between economic and personal stress, and take preventive steps to weaken the chain.

*   *   *

Agencies stay open longer. They've known that human service work is not 9-to-5, because in more cases than not the crisis calls come precisely when day shift workers (including those now calling) have gone home.

But now they move beyond knowing. They stagger hours, work split shifts, do weekends on rotation. Someone is always available round the clock, if only by beeper. Better spread too thin than stand too pat.

*   *   *

They hire local. They want to employ people who know the community, who are known by it, who represent it well. They give preference to volunteers they've trained. Only when expertise is not locally available will they look outside.

*   *   *

They use the phone: go to phone school, listen to themselves on tape, record standard messages, upgrade their switchboards, run teleclasses, do telemarketing, combine client phone service with same-day postcard or letter follow-up, keep phone logs and use them for needs assessment and evaluation.

*　　*　　*

They cut office expenses by going into the neighborhoods, hanging out on streets if that's what it takes. They become (first) visible, (then) approachable, and (then) credible. They deliver neighborhood services, shifting from place to place like the agents they are.

They learn who the key contact people in the neighborhood are, who to hit up on what. They learn who has power, who has motivation, and who has both. And they learn what the present helping structure is — who is sought out, who will move without being asked. Their goal is not to disrupt this structure, but rather to reveal it, to strengthen it, to make it work better. They are flavor-enhancers, bringing out the natural ingredients.

*　　*　　*

And they train — training is much of what they're about. To quote from the *Manifesto of the Inter-Agency Training Collaborative*:

We have joined in a collaborative because each of us has limited resources and we need to use them as wisely as we can. By joining together, we can get more done.

Our common goal is to empower the people we serve. To some, empowerment is a buzz word. To us, empowerment means self-confidence plus skills plus the motivation to use them. In other words, we want to help people shape their lives.

Our common method will be training, for that's largely how empowerment takes place.Our training philosophy is summarized in the 15 Principles below:

1. We will conduct systematic, quantitative, annual community needs assessments, and act on the results, really act. We will find out what kind of training is most needed, and then deliver it.

2. We will recruit the best trainers from all corners of town, or import them from outside if we have to. We will get especially tight with the local university, so that we can draw on their staff when there's need.

3. We will release agency staff time for training as necessary. (The collaborative's Training Board will process requests and resolve inequities.)

4. We will study conference planning and adult education techniques. We'll test almost anything once. But we'll deliver nothing without convincing trial runs, adequate preparation time, and the right training gear.

5. We will offer different training formats for different training needs: lectures and discussions; seminars and workshops; roundtables and forums; slide shows and cocktail hours; convocations and assemblies; retreats and parties; self-help fairs. We'll vary the length: one-shots or forevers. Your place or ours.

6. We will set behavioral objectives for each training event and keep them out front.

7. Some training will be aimed at the general public, and some to predetermined target groups. But in both cases we will market our programs aggressively, so that we get the audience we deserve.

8. We will charge what the traffic will bear for those who can bear it, but no one will ever be turned away for lack of cash. We'll defer payment, barter for time, accept donations to the Skills Exchange, or just waive it.

9. We will place a premium on training people to train others, for this is particularly cost-effective use of time. Then we'll follow up to check if they do.

10. And we will emphasize the training of gatekeepers, people who are already helping others, people already involved in natural helping networks, as the jargon phrase goes. This includes scout leaders, storekeepers, police, fire fighters, security guards, service reps, lawyers, folk healers, telephone operators, bartenders, barbers, beauticians, secretaries, receptionists, teachers, public officials, crime bosses, ministers, reporters, coaches, postal carriers, nursing home staff, cab drivers, club officers, business executives, real estate agents. There are many gatekeepers, for in our society there are many gates.

We will teach these gatekeepers about listening, about when to keep silent and when to intervene, how to respond supportively, how to make suggestions, and how and when to refer elsewhere. We will teach these gatekeepers advanced gate control, and give them a lot of support themselves, and make them feel important, for they are.

11. We will bring in gatekeepers to train agency staffs, too, and hope that as a result both groups will become a little more humble.

12. Training in and for neighborhoods will be essential, for the neighborhood is a primary locus of community action. We will do requests. But we will also develop standard program packages in: a. leadership skills development
   b. support group operation
   c. conflict mediation
   d. volunteer counselor training
   e. self-confidence
which we see as five areas of broadest applicability.

13. We will stock up on certificates, and pass them out liberally after training completion. We'll arrange with local colleges for partial course credits. And in any case we'll record continuing education units (which are being honored by more employers now as criteria for hiring and promotion), according to the formula worked out by the statewide training association.

14. We will evaluate whatever we do, formally, informally, verbally, and in writing. We'll go over the evaluations at a sit-down session and use them to improve. We'll never repeat anything without a numerical passing grade, at least not the same way.

15. Finally, we will collect new program ideas and general suggestions from all our training events and from our dream laboratories and bring them back to our home agencies for discussion and possible use in the future.

Through these Principles, we hope that agencies will be less like foreigners in the community. We hope to reduce our ignorance and insularity. We want community people to know us, to trust us, to call on us for the things we do well.

And we want people to go back to their neighborhoods and work settings with new skills and mindsets they can and will use in their daily lives. This will expand their community power, as well as their partnership with those who trained them. That's the whole point; for we in agencies must become partners in power with people we serve, working together for the common good.

*   *   *

The inter-agency splash party is about to begin. Once a year, on a late spring evening, down by the lake. A great chance to do no business, to shed layers of stiffness, to get to know each other as people, as brothers and sisters with skin.

*   *   *

As a splash-off, the service agencies in town develop a loose association. Once a month, whoever is free brings brown bags for lunch. There's maybe a few minutes of agenda, but most of it is shop talk, gossip, trading of bits and pieces, drifting off into topics unrelated to work at all. Over time, the lunchmates come to know, like, and trust each other, and look forward to getting together.

Another monthly meeting is more serious. It's an inter-agency planning meeting, designed to coordinate and improve services around town. There's a preset agenda, a rotating chair. Sometimes a client case is raised; planning for that person takes place on the spot. Other times, there's a discussion of potential joint projects and review of those projects already in place.

*   *   *

The inter-agency newsletter supplements the meeting goings-on. There are funding updates, and exposés. In the Idea Corner, someone writes: "People needing help often don't know where to turn, or have trouble picking up the phone, or both. Why don't we give them *one* number to call? Start a central intake, pool some staffing, tell them the information straight out, and if necessary refer them to a specific agency and person. I'd bet we'd provide better service for less money."

*   *   *

Agencies sit down with the telephone company. They figure that if there can be a yellow pages for commercial listings, why not a green pages for nonprofits? Bell says that if they don't profit, we won't either.

One Bell affiliate says we can't give you green. But we will print a self-help directory on the inside front cover, neighborhood offices as well, and we'll make sure each agency gets listed several times for the price of one. In return, we'd like you to give a workshop for our directory assistance operators.

The company also donates a WATS line to the Self-Help Clearinghouse, in accordance with the guidelines of its phone scholarship fund.

*   *   *

More inroads: A jointly-hired planner, and evaluator. A shared bookkeeper, and auditor. Shared use of office equipment. Shared office space, at least for some. Tentatively, a shared clinical specialist.

A while ago, the typist at one of the agencies was out sick for a few months. The stricken agency felt comfortable about asking its allies to pick up some of the clerical work. They said sure. One of these days, they'll need some help themselves. But that was a first.

*   *   *

Through their association, the agencies gain political clout. They get behind candidates for local office. The hiring of the town social services coordinator was originally their idea. A while ago, they successfully lobbied for small increases in town funding. They tend to get what they want because they are credible; they deliver; and they also target in on areas of their own duplication, where money can be saved.

*   *   *

Finally, the inter-agency group becomes a Council. The Council incorporates, gains nonprofit status, opens up consumer seats. It gets serious.

It asks for five percent of each agency's operating budget, and promises a return. Then it starts collaborative and sometimes money-making projects of its own: a rooming house visitation program; a multi-service center; business and industry consultation; the corporate saints and sinners; display advertisements; an all-citizen Human Services Committee; a local planning and budgeting manual; a community picnic; used car sales; an ethnic covenant; selective real estate investments...

*   *   *   *   *

*

*　　*　　*

*

One retired man, bored, looking for a way to pass the time. Finds there are more volunteer needs than he ever knew existed. Gets angry at himself and at others who are sitting around watching their hair grow grey. Makes himself a central source of volunteer opportunities. First, a little legwork. Then agencies, other organizations, sometimes even individuals who need work done call him at home. People with time on their hands call in too. A trickle at first, which is okay.

The coordinator matches work to worker, follows up each time. After a while (he keeps statistics), he worms into a back room at Town Hall. More people drop by to see him; he becomes an informal information and referral service. That is, he and his two buddies who come in to handle the phones and the paperwork when fish are biting.

The volume of calls is steady but slow. Eighty percent of the service comes from twenty percent of the people — what else is new? The other eighty percent need incentive; but what incentive will work if civic pride, social obligation, and personal recognition fall short, and you can't pay them? How about tax credits?

The coordinator introduces a proposal through town government: anyone performing X hours a week volunteer service for a registered nonprofit organization will receive a credit worth $Y on his municipal income tax. The proposal makes it through on the third try.

The number of calls to the Volunteer Office (new name) triples. About one percent of tax revenue is lost. The community gains several thousand hours a year of volunteer service. Is it worth it?

The coordinator makes out pretty well personally. It's nice for old folks to get a break.

*

*　　*　　*

*

support groups

This is me in my community:

I'm the filled-in circle. Everyone else looks wide open.

I can't exist by myself alone. I need connections with others to survive. I depend on others for my physical needs; sometimes these people live far away.

But I need people in my home community too. Their company opens my heart. I need people to say hello to me, to wave at me in the street, to feel close to and intimate with, to love and be loved by, to learn from, to give to, to teach, to serve, to do favors for me, to pick me up when I'm down, to affirm my worth, to help me grow. I need a network of people for all of these things.

Without my network, I would sink like a stone.

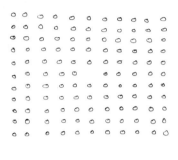

My network looks like this: There's my family and friends, right nearby. I have pretty good relations at work; they're included as well. I've sketched in my connections with my church, and in spring and summer I'm part of a Sunday evening softball game.

You can see that some of the people I'm connected to are also connected to each other, which is as it should be:

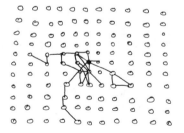

If you asked me, I'd say I'm happy, but deep down I know I'm looking for more. I'd like to feel closer to people. I'd like to give more love than I'm giving. I'd really like my network to look like this:

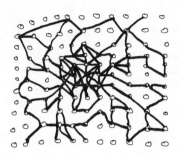

The stronger my network, the more black lines, the more supported I feel. I have a base for reaching my potential. I am secure; I have options; I know I won't fall too far.

And the stronger the connections among different members of the community, the stronger the supports for everyone, the better the community will be. Creating stronger connections is largely what these dreams are about.

* * *

Max's story: "Three months ago I joined the Men's Center and I stopped needing a cup cake and milk before bed."

* * *

To extend my support system, I can hook up with any number of groups in my community. There are brand-name associations and organizations, plus local clubs, churches, committees, and coffee klatsches. I can hold court by the park bench, or join some seekers of the higher good. It's just a question of my time and interest.

But sometimes none of these groups is what I need. I may want to talk about ideas and feelings with people who share my own special life concerns, who can understand me and help me as no other group can. That is, I may want to join a self-help group, or support group, whatever the current name.

•   •   •

Among the main support group listings at the Self-Help Clearinghouse:

Abortion
Abused children
Abused parents
Abusing parents
Adopted children

Adopting parents
Alcoholics
Anorexics
Assertiveness trainees
Bald people

Battered persons
Battering persons
Bereaved
Bleeding hearts
Blind persons

Block groups
Bulimics
Burn victims
Caesarean birth
Career changers

Children molested by parents
Children of separated or
    divorced parents
Children with aging parents
Coffee drinkers

Coma victims
Cooperatives
Crime victims
Cult members
Deaf persons

Debtors
Diseases:
    (acoustic neuroma
    ...venereal disease)
Divorced persons

Drug users
Emotional problems
Engaged couples
Epileptics
Ethnic groups

Ex-...
Exchanges
Exercisers
Families
Fathers for equal justice

Fathers of...
Fired workers
Football spouses
Foster parents
Friends of...

Gamblers
Gay couples
Gay fathers
Gay men
Gay mothers

Gay women
Genetic defects
Grandparents
Handicapped adults
Handicapped children

Hobby groups
Homemakers
Home workers
Incest
Infertility

Insomniacs
Intellectually gifted
Interracial couples
Job-finders
Juvenile offenders

Laid-off workers
Learning disabled
Left-handers
Little people
Married couples

Meditators
Men
Menopausal women
Military families
Mistresses

Mothers of...
Mothers without custody
Neighborhood groups
Newcomers
Nursing home groups

Nursing mothers
Orphans
Overeaters
Parents of ... children
Phobics

Pregnancy
Prisoners
Racial groups
Rape victims
Rejected authors

Retarded children
Runaways
Self-employed
Seniors
Separated persons

Sex offenders
Single men
Single parents
Single women
Skill-teaching groups

Smokers
Special interest groups
Stepchildren
Stepparents
Students

Stutterers	Veterans
Suicide attempters	Victorian homeowners
Teen-agers	Voluntarily childless couples
Tenants	Welfare recipients
Transients	Widowers
Transvestites	Widows
Under-employed	Women
Unemployed	Workaholics
Unmarried couples	Working couples
Vegetarians	Young executives

These are cross-indexed, and subdivided by type. You call up, ask for what you want, and get information and referral over the phone. Or you can write a letter. Or come in and examine their files, which are open to the public.

Most groups meet regularly, some only from time to time. Some rarely get together as a full group, but just knowing about other people out there with the same issues as you, whom you can find if you need them, can give you intangible support.

Some put out reading lists. Some give courses, and hold training programs of their own. Some run little ads under the heading "New Groups Starting," which the papers print weekly. Some have newsletters, and self-help guides. Some have small working libraries. Some engage in advocacy. Some push for legislation. Some do community education and public relations drives and fund raising. Some will give you contacts you can talk to over the phone, or live people you can lean on in a crisis.

Some are therapy groups, acknowledged or not. Some are for intimates of people in distress. Some are social action groups, where support is a by-product. Some are social clubs, pure and simple. Some are casual yet potent groups, which may not even think of themselves as groups as such, and which would never be listed in an open file were it not for the thoroughness of the Clearinghouse researchers.

If you're looking for a group but can't find the one you want, put your name and interest down under "Situations Wanted." If others call in, or respond to the monthly bulletin, the Clearinghouse will contact all of you so you can get together.

And if you want to start your own group or chapter, the Clearinghouse will help you get under way. It conducts training programs, workshops, open houses of its own, as well as supplying consultation on a time-unlimited basis.

The support groups listed are loose and structured, authoritarian and anarchic, open and closed. They have different memberships, expectations, geographies, meeting frequencies, turnover rates, degrees of permanence, and so on. Yet once consciousness about supports is raised, it's a little easier for people to seek out help from each other, whether through the Clearinghouse or not.

*　　*　　*

People who have pledged to help other people wear fish pins on their clothing. They have sworn to stop for stranded motorists, give handouts to drunks, carry umbrellas on cloudy days, and watch for situations where they can give their reasonable best. All right, we'll agree that people in distress can wear fish belly up.

*　　*　　*

The mental health center sends a fellow around to make contact with the high-tech people in his area.
What on earth for?
Maybe they can pool resources, support each other, work for a common cause.
What would it be? And how do you network high tech?

We're not entirely clear how; but maybe if we are enthusiastic and sincere and if we can get people talking together, it will lead to something. High tech might feel isolated. Also, we have to start somewhere.

*　　*　　*

In rural areas, city shrinks work with locals in groups of ten, trying to open them up. Small-town life can wear at the gums. How can we get people not to be so goddamn *nice* to each other? How can we cut through the decency and uprightness, releasing the growth energy from the cruel and hateful?

*   *   *   *   *

festivals

On January 1, 2000, each person in the world reaches out to hold the hands of two others. Crowds form in the streets, no circles allowed. Through global accord, they stand for five minutes and let the energy flow through. Some cry; some won't let go.

*   *   *

Waldo County, Maine: The Cabin Fever Reliever in February brings frozen residents out of their homes. A variety show and binge following takes out some of the kinks and quiets the devils.

*   *   *

Smaller parties, throughout the year. Impromptu cookouts. Victorian parties, Elizabethan, medieval, Greek, Roman, toga, Egyptian, flaunt your cultural heritage, revolutionary, anarchist, antebellum, D/depression, day after you died, pumpkin and Christmas, riverfront and cherry blossom, full moon. Expositions, Crazy Days, Centennial Days, Historical Days, feast days, homecomings, and progressive dinners. Parties to celebrate the saints and those who should have been. Parties to welcome the seasons, the vernal and autumnal equinoxes, the summer and winter solstices, crossings and transits. Honoring the harvest and the harvest moon. Upfront paganism, placing self in tune with nature.

* * *

Boston, New Year's Eve: Hundreds of entertainers have come downtown to bring in the New Year. There are almost 100 separate performances throughout the evening in more than two dozen locations, starting at dusk, continuing till the *Times* ball drops at midnight. Admission to all events is by button, available at nominal cost. In the dark and cold, thousands of households walk the streets and wish each other happiness.

* * *

Gilroy, Calif.: "The site selected for the first Garlic Festival was a privately-owned ranch on Highway 101. There were, in all, 70 booths, most of them related to garlic in one way or another. Booths were decorated with braids of garlic. The Fresh Garlic Association had a booth with information about garlic and garlic growing. One booth sold odorless garlic in a variety of forms. Another sold garlic pills for the relief of high blood pressure. This was in addition to the food of Gourmet Alley, Italian sausages, garlic-braised meats, tostadas, lumpia.... *The Los Angeles Herald-Examiner* commented, 'Vendors held to the basic theme, offering an eye-watering array.' No one knows for sure how many persons attended. 'Only 15,000 tickets were printed; after that things got a little loose.' "

* * *

An eminent sociologist: "Block parties are typical late-in-the-day desperate attempts at community building. Next to the singles' bars, I don't know of anything more shallow. People get together in the streets for a few hours of excitement and then the whole thing disappears."

* * * * * * * * *

Bugles blow at dawn on Town Day. Riders on horseback gallop through the streets. Get ready; get ready.

Everybody in town is in the Apache relay. Odd-numbered street addresses are the Greens; evens are the Golds, the town colors. Everyone three and over has a task to do, on a master list sent by mail and kept on record. The whistle blows: the three-year-olds are off, running 20 yards and passing green or gold batons to the next youngster down the line. The fours and fives will run further. School-age children have different tasks to do: eating peanut-butter sandwiches (no milk); digging a one-foot hole; climbing a ten-foot rope; catching a butterfly!

The participants get older, and the relay moves on, neither team able to take a clear lead. The pledge of allegiance is recited backwards. Twenty anagrams to "Apache Indians" are uncovered. Five foul shots are tossed through the hoop. Teen-age runners do two laps around the track, or hop backwards down Main Street, or pull each other in red wagons. Crowds follow everywhere, as the relayers wind through every street in town.

The race ends up by the waterfront. Speedboats roar around the lake. Then waders reach out to swimmers, who bring the batons out to high divers, who leap toward surfboarders who sprint out to war canoes poised a quarter mile away. Two canoes paddle furiously back to shore. The first one back on land wins the race. Gunwale to gunwale, bow to bow. Throngs of spectators are cheering from the beach. The Greens touch first this year; breakfast is on them.

Ten thousand pancakes have been flipped for the occasion. Coffee in vats the size of oil drums. Greens and their gold mates, now shorn of color identities, sit down to eat together. There is a prayer. After breakfast, the convocation begins.

The whole town turns out for the convocation. Just seeing everyone gathered together is exciting. The color guard marches down the avenue bearing the American flag, the state flag, the flags of neighborhood and town. The mayor bids welcome. The ministers give a joint invocation. The gold-etched scroll with the story of the town is taken from its vault and read aloud by the Historian — most people know it by heart, but this is ceremony, and it's nobly written. Awards are presented, for the most valuable community program and the most improved neighborhood. For the most useful invention, and the most practical joke. For distinguished community service, as well as for Renaissance man and woman of the year, celebrating the all-around person. The winners of the town competitions in literature, fine arts, social philosophy, and applied science are announced and honored. A cheer goes up as those most recently elected to the town hall of fame are formally inducted.

Randomly chosen representatives from the town at large make short remarks on topics of their choice. A longer address is given by the invited speaker, as in college commencements. A torchbearer lights the community flame. The flags are raised. The people sing "God Bless America" and the "Internationale" and join hands for the town anthem. The band breaks into Dixieland; now the party has begun.

There is carnival, bacchanal, fiesta. Every street, every block on every street, is decked out double. Banners and bunting, placards and streamers, balloons, clowns, and confetti showers. Marching bands, conga lines, drum and bugle corps weave in and out in their own time. Floats from every group in town roll by, few without secret surprises.

In the four corners of the town, more bands, playing polkas, hard rock, West Indian, and swing. A gigantic earthball careens down the street, chased by swarms of kids. Giant puppets on stilts, storytellers who carve out corners, street poets passing out broadsides. All cops on duty have red noses today. Most have the day off, for today is one of liberty if not justice for all.

The exposition grounds this year feature the double-Dutch jumprope competition, a lima-bean-eating contest, a make-your-own-town-mural, a historical scavenger hunt, the golden age olympics, a hot-air balloon launch, a parachute landing, the disabled veterans parade, spitting for distance, frisbee tossing, long-distance marble shooting, new games, just-invented games, Johnny-on-the-pony, the interscholastic tug of war, Dunk the Commissioner, King of the Mudflats, home chemistry demonstrations, free hug coupons, edible sculpture, a community fish fry, open microphones, card sharps, roving photographers, folk choreographers, costume galleries, Wonder Women with lassoes, tots' tricycle races, the celebrity auction, the nostalgia quiz, arm wrestling, thumb wrestling, strawberry jello wrestling, the strongest man and woman, and the sexiest young and old couples judging.

The a cappella chorus goes caroling, since it's back from tour. The community networker is around making connections. Once again, there'll be an attempt to break the Guinness record for the largest game ever of musical chairs.

On stage: the grade school spelling bee; a yo-yo exhibition; disappearing rabbits; a local acrobatic troupe; the average body pageant; the hidden talent show; the Sweet Adelines; the tall story hour; straight and punk fashion tryouts; the public servants' extravaganza.

Wandering around, food stalls of every description. Outdoor haircuts, dog grooming, car washes. Bob for apples; knock over the milk containers; send your friend a kiss by proxy. Everything's free today. A pickup game of Steal the Bacon. Oriental kite flying. Life-size monopoly. The agencies and self-help groups beckon from their booths. Streams of adults and kids in different color T-shirts chase after each other in city-limits Capture the Flag.

A silversmith has sculpted an Indian figure, reflecting the town's early heritage. On Town Day, the Indian is hidden out of doors, somewhere above ground. Who will find it?

A Main Street walker might get hit by a pie or by a jumping frog; might consult the Imperial Wizard or spin the Wheel of Life; might jump on the hay wagon or ride the elephant or the camel who are out of jail free. Everyone seems to be an astrologer, troubadour, leprechaun, or oracle. Between the prize-winning sheep and the giant cucumbers, psychologists and social workers vie for the most helpful answers to your personal problems. The face painter uses only psychic colors. The gynecologist dispenses sex information. The balloon man meets up with the pin lady. The governor puts away a few beers, refuses ethnic food; later on tours the Life Maze exhibit, representing the six stages of moral development.

At the fair, will you be a water balloon bomber? Will you umpire the Unitarians vs. Baptists softball game? Will you draw a new town logo? Will you dare to enter the hot tub tent?

This afternoon's events (partial schedule):

1:00 Underwater music concert
1:30 Bike-in movies, kids only
2:00 Haunted house opens up
2:30 Jousting tournament, in the stadium
      (with Encounterbats)
3:00 Medals handed out, your choice of
      engraving
3:30 Burying of the time capsule
4:00 Glass bottle launch, by the river
4:30 Tag team log rolling
5:00 Non-stop sock hop
5:30 The great tomato war

Thousands of people bring dishes to the world's largest potluck. Pheasant under glass. Chicken casseroles. Roast pigs on spits. Roast ox on pylons. Jambalayas, rijstaffels, pâtés, chili dogs, nouvelle cuisine, Tex-Mex, bouillabaisses, minestrones, paellas, bourgignons, stroganoffs, carbonades, choucroutes, cacciatorres, schnitzels, chicken-fried, hash browns, flambés, jello molds, almondines, florentines, marsalas, scallopines, bean dips, parmigianas, curries, moles, pilafs, aspics, Stouffer's fettucini, chef's, caesar, and Waldorf salads, sourdoughs, deep dishes, pan dowdies, sfogliatellis, upside-downs, mousses, tortes, bombes, coupes, zabagliones, rice puddings, oatmeal cookies, double chocolates, and meringues. One day a year, so line up and dig in. Clydesdale horses pull up with the beer wagon. Ronald McDonald cruises with laced orange drink.

At dusk, the masked ball begins. Main Street is blocked off — no admittance without full costume, The masquerade has started. Dancing to waltzes and to old-time hits from the Golden Treasury. The air is redolent with courtliness and charm. The band asks the dancers to join in, and two thousand masked men and women sing. Prizes are given as the dance winds down: if you recognize your neighbor, let him know, and he is out, or vice versa. Don't guess wrong, for that's your elimination. The last couple to be tapped are

King and Queen of the ball. They mount the stage, as familiar voices shout congratulations.

A fireworks display co-sponsored by the cooperative savings bank and competing units of the National Guard and the U.S. Army Corps of Engineers, which are looking for something to do on weekends. Every degree of sky lights up, while the band plays on.

Midnight, masks come off. Torchlight processions back to the neighborhoods. Block parties are gearing up. Intimate parties, if you care to go. Smaller pickup bands. Toss all the kids' shoes into one big outdoor pile. Build a bonfire in the middle of the block and toast marshmallows. Make your own music. Pass around the good stuff. Sleep when you must. The pancake makers are back at their trade, mixing batter for those who will still be awake at the second dawn.

On the Sabbath, it is quiet. The stores are closed. Most people stay around and save gas. They visit each other, go to church, walk in the woods, and reflect. They are renewed.

* * * * *

media

Home from work...Let's see what's happening this week...

Leafing through the newspaper, the reader finds:

• A debate on a current local issue. The publishers have long believed that truth is revealed by bringing opponents together and letting them have at each other. So issues are posed, and debaters invited. Sparks are supposed to fly, though the 55-decibel limit is enforced. The debates used to go on at the newspaper office before they moved to the auditorium and opened up to the public. Next week's edition prints the transcript in full.

• Reader comments on an issue the editors have posed. Should we shut the adult bookstore, or subsidize the industrial park? The editorial staff supplied some background in last week's paper, printed a boxed summary of pros and cons, proposed tentative weightings of criteria, and said come on, folks, let's hear from you. This week, a full page of comment on that issue alone. When issues are scarce, they are created. The editor-in-chief, pedagogue that she is, often resorts to pump-priming to get thought flowing.

• Results of a newspaper poll. The editorial staff raises a question, sometimes on reader request. Two phone lines are open. The ayes call one, the nays another. Votes are tallied and published, along with representative comments.

(One time the paper boys and girls went around with survey forms the paper printed up, then collected them the next week, on their next time back. The paper trained the kids in basic door-to-door technique, and gave out bonuses for 100% compliance.)

• An expanded letters to the editor section, another pet project. The editor believes in print literacy, spurs letter-writing assignments in the schools, is known to pay postage due. No libel, and only one sheet of paper, but otherwise everything goes in.

• A guest column, by any citizen, on a topic of concern at least to him or her. Usually there's at least one per issue. Anybody can write a guest column, on just about anything, up to the three-a-year limit. All you do is call in to reserve, and sign youself up on the waiting list if necessary.

• News: Neighborhood stringers send in field reports. (The neighborhood newsletter got started when one stringer flooded the copy desk.) The paper also has a standing policy of printing all releases it receives, lightly edited and usually unabridged. The aim is to have half the column inches home spun.

• The declassifieds, where many people look first, and which have become sort of a community bulletin board instead of an afterthought.

. Anyone with a free item or service can have it listed gratis under "What's for Free." A lot of stuff that would normally get tossed with the trash gets picked up this way. Town departments advertise, and are not above responding to ads either.

. If you don't want to give it away, there's a separate heading for "Bargain Items under $10.00." These ads are free, too. (The big-ticket ads, though, work on honor-system commission; more revenue that way.)

Other free ad sections:

Jobs wanted:	by kids over 16
	by people over 65
	by newly-released prisoners
	by anyone who's unemployed
Lost ads:	(sympathy is expressed; blame is not presumed)
Found ads:	(finders get a free ad credit)

All these media freebees pay off in higher circulation, which means higher advertising rates off a broader readership base. Also, subscribers get three free ads a year, which turns out to be a nice incentive.

• The personals ads, which do cost. These are usually people wanting to meet people, with box numbers, carefully screened. Pure or reasonably pure intentions only.

• Responses to the suggestion contest. Every so often, a query: "What's the best way to...?" Cash prizes for the three best suggestions, as judged by an independent committee. Any suggestion made gets printed up and replied to, no matter how far out, as long as there's a name. This becomes one of the most cost-effective programs going. Once in a while, publicized bids for inventions, open RFP's taken out of the small print. From time to time, contests for the best new question.

• "Confidential Chat." Here people share feelings anonymously, using pen names. Here they deal with problems of living, not social issues of the day. Chatters write in with "What do I do now?" Others respond with their empathic best. Many have been there.

• The news in Spanish. We live in a multi-ethnic country, and bilingual education cuts two ways. A little grammar instruction, and a short word list each week.

• A How-to series, teaching skills of modern life not all of us have. How to secure your home against intruders. How to cut your own hair. How to drive in snow and ice. How to write a résumé, arrange for a funeral, get a bank loan, and so on. A reprint list is available; send a SASE.

• A Kids' Corner, written by kids, for and about. Stories, puzzles, cries of injustice, negotiation strategies, legislative updates, after-school possibilities, events this weekend, who's sleeping over where. An outlet for classroom creativity beyond purple ink. Their own office suite at the paper downtown also helps them value journalism more.

• Volunteer opportunities, solicited by the newspaper itself.

• A community calendar: what's going on around town this week. Arranged first by type of event, then separately by day, time, and place, with numbers to call for further details. The most obscure organizations get first billing. Also, coming events, and live possibilities, contingent on interest.

The editors think that the newspaper should serve as reporter and also as critic, as community builder and also as building inspector. Their philosophy is if you read the local paper, you are going to know what community you are living in, and how to make it better.

•   •   •

The Home and Garden Editor, he who sits by the phone, tells his colleagues. The Food Editor takes a turn another day. Sports the next. Future topics: legal aid, travel, pet care, investments, if they can find the right staff or sign on some experts. One caller asks why don't they take their calls live over the radio?

Once a week a staffer puts together a two-hour digest of the week's news on a cassette and sends copies to the school for the blind, the library, a few private subscribers. Once a month, there's a personal school visit, a talk and discussion; a way of keeping current. They suggest a daily taped edition. Maybe we can, and maybe you'd like to help.

The big-city newspaper also helps out neighborhood, school, and ethnic weeklies. Workshops on investigative reporting, on layout, on circulation and promotion. Page-by-page critiques. A few summer internships for bright school kids, and others who apply. Some back-and-forth tips on specific advertisers, on the assumption that there'll be enough ad income to go around.

* * *

While the newspaper founder eventually sold the paper to its Community Advisory Board, the local radio station was publicly owned from the start. Nearly half its revenue comes from listener contributions. Each contributing member can vote for the Board of Directors, regardless of dollar amount given. The Board solicits program ideas and controls program content. It's a commercial station, equally committed to making waves and staying afloat.

So the listener hears news, sports, weather, and happy music, but also high school radio drama, trials in progress, next week in review, and streetcorner debates wired in. Some of the programming overlaps with the newspaper — the citizen editorials, the call-in shows, and so on — for some people are more attuned to audio channels. But some is more original: the bird song hour, city council meetings, voices behind prison walls, and a muckraking feature of the week, live and remote. All of this depends on decent ratings, and the station does its own personal checking, which is also determination of need. The good stuff of more than local interest gets regionally syndicated.

* * *

There'll never be a shortage of people with problems. The talk-show host is a skilled clinician, who knows what can be done over the airwaves and what can't. He knows when to intervene, how to probe, when to keep silent, where to refer. Since the show is part of his work week at the mental health center, among other things it helps bring agency and community closer together.

* * *

Nine p.m. is for "Connections." Call up and describe yourself and the person you'd like to meet. For example, in abridged form:

Phil, 5'10", 165, 37, non-smoking, light-drinking professional man, recently single, likes quiet walks, modern jazz, Chinese food, is looking to meet a career-directed, non-smoking woman, 30-40, who values closeness and independence and shares his tastes, for companionship and possibly a more lasting relationship....

First names only. The host will ask you a question or two and give you a box number. The next day, sift through the messages from all those who'd like to know you better.

*   *   *

Reading aloud from novels, the classics yet, and just before bedtime. But the classics are soothing, like a warm glass of milk. When read well, they unplug you from the world, and still they glorify. Listeners report addiction, leading to TV exile.

*   *   *

Local cable picks up where radio leaves off. Before the community access channel started teaching the public how to use the equipment, video games competitions got top billing. But now, with trained crews vying for air time, we get legislative hearings with color commentary, close-up livestock judging, and the pool hall championships with reverse angle replay. Watch the camera work on the exterior painting demonstrations, and the fancy lead-ins to the astrological forecast. Plus the job ads, racing odds, language labs, teen fashions, stock predictions, store specials, and voting at home (Tuesday nights). In the small towns, where cable doesn't reach, low-power TV stations cover much the same ground.

Cable produces its own soap operas to reinforce multiple role models. A prime-time favorite is Jane Doe, District Attorney.

*   *   *

The local media collaborate and form a Media Center. The community's film library and tape archives are housed over there.

At the Center, newspaper, radio, and television staff share their skills, with university input as well. Most organizations, for example, have learned by now to create slide-tape shows for promoting their own causes. Some make video tapes, while others produce short subjects or community newsreels, shown before the main feature at local movie houses. Workshops are offered in video conferencing, voice mail, CB applications, talk-back cable, and other edges of the art. The posters around town, collector's items now, get shown in retrospective.

*   *   *

Baltimore: "For four hours on radio station WBAL, Mayor William Schaefer and police officials took calls in a program called 'Report a Pusher.' They say they got 'quality information' as listeners reported license numbers of cars, described times and locations of drug transactions and names of buyers and sellers. The program brought 250 calls and led to 91 arrests...."

*   *   *

Fall River, Mass.: Jan's Polish Kitchen is on the air. The only place in town where you can learn to make pirogies and gablicka in the privacy of your own home, share your family recipes with others, and hear what's going on in the Polish community. Commercial TV beckons, but Jan has decided she's going to stay small and homey.

*   *   *   *   *

information

In the bowels of the town hall, or in the corner of the general store, or at the switchboard of the police department, or behind the desk at the youth center, or at a kitchen table, but eventually in a welcoming and sunny office, the community information specialist sits. Her job is to know everything going on in town and to dispense such knowledge on request.

Reference materials are at the ready. On nearby shelves are town reports by department; budgets by year; inventories of municipally-owned equipment; names and numbers of town employees; descriptions of helping agencies and the services they provide; the same for community organizations and ad hoc groups, all with contact persons; business and professional directories; a map collection; a street atlas; criss-cross phone books; U.S. census block statistics; voting lists; school catalogs and yearbooks; audit reports; back issues of the local paper with an indexed clip file; restaurant menus; school lunches; tonight's performers; lists of churches, nursing homes, secretarial schools, and technical training institutes; folders full of clubs, women's groups, and youth leaders; and homemade trouble-shooting guides, over and beyond what is found anywhere else, and more up to date. All of this is standard by now, the limbs of the system.

The heart is inside the specialist's head. Her brain cells are little Rolodexes. Precisely because it's her job to know everything that's happening, and not to make policy decisions, she does know. And she knows also that knowledge is power, and she is wise enough to realize how much power she has, and smart enough to keep this realization pretty much to herself, for otherwise she could easily get in big trouble.

She does know. She knows what people will go out of their way to be helpful, and who will be rude as usual. She knows where to find a lawyer on 24-hour call, who is good at getting squirrels out of the attic, who can interpret in Vietnamese, and what auto body shops will give you the best all-around deal. She knows these things from having lived 30 or 40 or 50 years in the community; they are etched in her being. When she doesn't know herself, she is likely to know someone who does, or at the very least to know someone who is one or more steps closer to the answer.

In nice weather, she moves to a kiosk on the main square, sometimes sitting by a table outside. Being the most knowledgeable person around, it's right she should be most central. She becomes town greeter as well, though reminding herself to send tourists to the visitor center across the way.

When it's dark, the night mayor assumes her functions, for being an information specialist is also a moonlight job.

In her own annual report, justifying next year's budget appropriation, she writes: "There are plenty of resources and services in the community. Granted, maybe not enough. But I'm here because most of the people most of the time have only the faintest conception of what's going on.

"My job is to make facts flow freely, for wide-open communication channels precede a cohesive community. What's more, I'm giving inservice training in community resources to other town staff as part of their orientation. I've begun consultation with some community groups as well. Two years from now, I plan to have accomplished most of my goals, and then you can cut this position back to half time."

*   *   *

Skills Bank
Application Form

Voluntary Action Center
of
Middleburg County

Name: John Smithers   Date: 10/2/84

Current Street Address: 412 Spruce St.   Day telephone: (601) 993-7000

City: Middleburg   State Zip Code: MS 39309   Evening telephone: (601) 214-5203

Occupation or career field (if student, year and major): Chemical Engineer   Age: 38

SKILLS & INTERESTS   Drawing from the attached list of skill categories, write below those you most want to involve in this program. Add your own categories if you wish.

Basketball   Photography   Chemistry
Sports officiating   Environmental Planning   Pharmacology
Vocational Ed.   Intercultural Exchanges   Math tutor
Solar Energy   _____   _____
_____   _____   _____

INVOLVEMENT PREFERENCES   How do you want to use your skills? Check all the appropriate boxes below.

[X] Teacher/Coach   [ ] Intern   [ ] Advocate on related issues

[X] Speaker   [ ] Workshop resource person   [ ] On-site consultant

[X] Counselor to individuals   [ ] Board member   [X] Evaluator

TIME AVAILABILITY FOR VOLUNTEER OPPORTUNITIES (Check all that apply)

[ ] Weekdays   [X] Week nights   [X] Weekends   [X] By appointment

FINANCIAL REQUIREMENTS (Check only one)

[ ] Must have salary   [X] Volunteer only   [ ] Salary or volunteer OK

COMMENTS: Write on back.

All of this was step one. When there was more loose information than could fit inside one head, a resident file system began. This was simple: A brightly-colored form got dropped by each resident's door. Side one listed skills; side two, interests. Residents checked off skills they'd be willing to share, plus interests they'd like to pursue, used the blank spaces for write-ins, signed their names, and sent the form back. All of this optional, no obligation, and free.

The forms returned were open-filed, so for those wanting lists of beekeepers or piano teachers or potential school bus drivers, all they had to do was look. Any further arrangements were individually negotiated.

*　　　*　　　*

One larger community, weighted with forms, went to edge-punched cards. The tools of this trade are some specially-printed cards with holes around the edges, a paper punch, and long knitting needles. The information on the form is hand-punched around the perimeter of the card according to a preset coding system. To retrieve it, just pass the needles through the proper holes in the stack, and the cards you want will simply drop out. The advantage of this system is its cross-indexing — you can tell very quickly how many gardeners live in a particular neighborhood, how many Methodists are also Kiwanis, or if any retired welders would like to make a comeback.

*　　　*　　　*

Big communities break the needles. Aren't you supposed to go to computers then? Well, maybe, sometimes. But if there are technical whizzes with time on their hands, that's an argument in favor.

Most of the skills, interest, and other resource data are plugged into the community data bank. Each neighborhood has a separate disk. You can visit the bank and the supervisor will show you how to get what you want, or handle your question personally. Or if you have a computer at home, you can punch in your request and get near-instant feedback right over the screen.

When hooked into local cable, the data bank adds event listings, ticket availabilities, library reserves, back paper copies, whatever is in demand. It evolves into a two-way bulletin board, a computer-age general store: Who wants a babysitter tonight? Can anyone lend me a stopwatch, or know where I can find one? Personal notes like this, every half-hour or so, in unending variety. You can pay your taxes, make an appointment at the beauty shop, or confirm your vacation plans. You can use the bank as a part-time dating service, or friendship bureau, since friends are harder to find.

The data bank is also a scientist's dream, for, consent being explicit, rarely have so many researchers had access to so much data so easily. The issue is one of using the data, and the technology, to improve the human condition.

.   •   •

If you have a community question, call the information specialist. If it deals with outside, try the reference librarian. And if you want a social service, call your broker. She's been hired collectively by all helping agencies in town to screen incoming calls and to direct callers to the right place.

But if you have a complaint, or a suggestion, or a compliment, contact the ombudsman. It's his job to record feedback and to respond to every comment made, investigating and mediating when necessary. If the phone lines are always busy, if a community employee was insulting over the phone, if the check was not really in the mail, he is the person to call for action. All complaints received, and that means all, are logged and individually reviewed at an executive meeting once a week. It's policy to respond to the caller informally within no more than 24 hours, and in writing in no more than 30 days.

•   •   •

The *Pocket Resource Guide*, fifth edition, is free on the streets. (Six panels; 100 names, addresses, and phones.) High school seniors get them on graduation. Newcomers find them in the mail. Politicians use them as campaign literature. Newspapers print a section a month. They'll reach every alley and farm, if meter readers agree. Inside, they'll go by the phone.

The guide is translated into other languages of the town. A large type edition for the elderly. Separate booklets for teens, for gays, for seniors, for widows, for cancer patients, for the disabled, for support group seekers, for other target groups. Some have Q.-and-A. sections attached, or other descriptive prose. A few have experimented with advertising. *Who's Who in Town Government* has mug shots and capsule bios.

Most people in town have copies of the general pocket guide and several special versions. If there's some redundancy, it's worth it. This is a well-informed community; no one can say that people don't know what's going on. They may not need the information now, but they have it, or know it's nearby.

* * *

Citizen groups borrow from these ideas. And they plant telephone trees, for welfare-checking as well as information-dispensing. When each person calls three others, ten branches will reach 59,049 twigs. This allows for some slippage.

* * *

When Spot got lost, Spot's owner thought it might be good if other pet losers and finders had a common place to call. One press release later, the Lost Pet Hotline was born. Only later did Spot's owner appreciate that "hotline" and "telephone" are almost the same, that any phone is a hotline if you want it to be.

Other hotlines fall into place. The jazzline. The jokeline. The sports line. The county line, for community support. The hotlines for road conditions and open gas stations, utility cutoffs and union news, pending legislation, and household hints. The vegetarian hotline proposes wholesome meals for the day. The elder service numbers — Lifeline, Telecare, reassurance, phone buddy — get special attention and publicity. Somewhere a child reads recorded messages of hope.

The community usually has a few dozen hotlines working at any one time. Some have beepers, for the insistent. They go in and out of business, waxing and waning with the laws of supply and demand. This is natural, all part of the process, grist for the mill.

* * *

From hotline to clearinghouse is one step up. You become a clearinghouse when you have a specialized concern plus the interest, plus some expertise to match. On government grants, for example, or herbal remedies, or solar access legislation, or something else which few people in the nation know about, and you do. Your fair share of audacity and ambition also helps.

The phone rings as the kids are tracking mud on the floor. "Hello, Spina Bifida Clearinghouse.... Will you guys get out of the kitchen? It's Kansas calling on the toll-free line..." This adds to the phone bill, but the Clearinghouse makes most of it back on newsletter subscriptions.

Sometimes city or state will share in the operation. Sometimes they'll hire their own experts to set them up. Sometimes, if the clearinghouse is sophisticated, it will do computer searches of the literature for you and mail you an annotated bibliography, the reasoning being that people should enjoy the fruits of modern technology.

*   *   *

Then there are tapes in the night, a library of recorded messages on the subject at hand. Pick up a program, place a call, tell the tape jockey what you want to hear, and he or she will slide it into the player. On health issues, mental health, tax preparation, the law for starters. You can take some courses by tape now; call the studio, ask for customer assistance.

*   *   *

The glossy magazine at the counter is a singles datebook. People still need intimacy, love, and a way to meet. Bars among other things are expensive. Datebook listings are free, a full paragraph of prose, arranged by sex and then geography. Pictures are optional. The magazine is respectable, and since advertisers have come knocking on the door, it figures to stay around for a while.

*   *   *

The transit authority donates advertising space to local nonprofits for informational messages. You'll find current events printed from time to time on milk cartons, posted on billboards, or written in the sky.

Other notices go out to the Thumbtack Bugle, a professional information-posting service. The bugle is for hire to hang your stuff or spread your leaflets in any legal place in town. Call up the bugler and customize your route, or choose from among three standard itineraries.

*   *   *

The community networker's ears have moved perceptibly closer to his head from spending so much time on the phone. His job is to make connections between one person and another. He knows who's doing what or who could. He refers, prompts, organizes, spurs on, plants seeds, and has a direct line to the cochlear nerve.

He's a dot-to-dot player, a community air traffic controller. Each cognitive flight, real or fancy, must reach its best destination. When someone calls, he works out the flight patterns. And when business is slow, he floats his own balloons. Everyone needs balloons, and flight plans.

*   *   *   *   *

libraries

This is brainstorm day at the library, where the staff assignment is to think of things customers might want to borrow. We already have books, a record collection, some art prints — what else?

"Cameras. (Use promo: 'We've got the cameras — get the picture?')"

"Puzzles — jigsaw, mechanical, three-dimensional, cube."

"Games — board games, strategy games, original games, instruction sheets for games to assemble yourself."

"Toys. Dolls."

"But no dolls that do more than bat their eyes."

"Objects. I mean like starfish, arrowheads, bird's nests, natural history stuff. Artifacts. Museum pieces to loan."

"Pets — well, maybe that is more hassle than it's worth."

"Museum passes — have the library belong to the local museums, so that people can borrow our membership card to get in for a day."

"Tickets to cultural events. We could buy some tickets to the ballet, symphony, repertory groups, and the ball teams."

"Kits, of books, magazines, toys, and puzzles, and activities for children who are sick at home, that their parents can take out for them."

"Hobby kits."

"Picnic kits, with outdoor play equipment."

"No, that idea has already gone out to the Recreation Department."

"Okay, I've got geological survey maps, street atlases, musical instruments, box turtles, tax forms, recipes, video cassettes, game cartridges, darkroom supplies, and camping equipment."

"Costume jewelry."

"Costumes in general. Fake furs."

"Rent out the whole library for fund-raising events."

"Rent out the librarians for fun-raising events!"

*   *   *

The library got into a shoving match with the tool-rental people when it began to loan out real tools. It figured that since tools are instruments of power, and since knowledge is power, therefore tools are instruments of knowledge. The tool-rental company claimed faulty reasoning and said that the library was cutting into its business. The library said who says we can't loan out tools, if that's what people want, and especially if they're donating used tools for our inventory.

Hopefully, a compromise will be reached. Meanwhile, enough people were interested in the tool-loaning concept to make it go, and so now it operates out of an old town garage, a "branch library," as a joint project with the Department of Public Works.

*   *   *

The library makes do in no small part through a vigorous and well-publicized book donations program. It has carefully-maintained pipelines for getting old Book-of-the-Month Club selections, college texts no longer matriculating, books purchased but never read, books borrowed but never returned, gift books never opened, well-read favorites, publishers' overstocks, other libraries' discards, promotional copies, books from estates, and bequests from people who are lightening up or moving on in life.

Every year the Library Friends sponsors Bookfinders Week, when citizens are urged to prune their shelves and comb their basements for whatever they can part with. Prizes of new hardcovers (winners' choice) are given to the top three contributors.

The library will take whatever it can get. Some books are healthy enough to go straight to the shelves. Others go downstairs to the processing room, where they are mended, or traded to other libraries, or sold to used-college-text houses, or shipped overseas as Books for Peace. Occasionally, one is sold to an antique bookdealer (donors waive claim to resale value). Whatever can't be used, fixed, traded, shipped, or sold is recycled into card stock.

The same goes, more or less, for games, puzzles, and records too. What else are kids going to do with their old stuff?

* * *

The town's oldest continuous book exchange takes place near the front steps. Twenty-four hours, at least in good weather. Bring in two, take out one. Separate sections for soft- and hardbacks. Unmarked books only, please, in halfway decent condition. Those which don't move after a while go on sale, Parisian style, in sidewalk bins, for pocket change.

* * *

In what used to be the director's office, there's now a cozy and tastefully-stocked bookstore. New titles same day out of the carton. Gift wrapping on request. It's a revenue-producing library function, and much of the revenue comes from coffee and the homemade pastries the retired librarian bakes and sells while she sits behind the counter chatting with customers and crocheting blankets for her grandchildren.

* * *

In the bowels of the library, copyreaders and indexers are working on contract. The Bookbinders stitch worn volumes to Schoenberg quartets. They keep old books in circulation, themselves as well.

* * *

As more people began to spend more time in their own communities, the library became more of a local cultural center. More bulletin boards for lectures, workshops, service offerings, event notices. More varied exhibits in the cases in the foyer. More demand on the meeting rooms, and rooms which were never used for meetings or which were hardly rooms at all got pressed into service. The Adult Education Center taught courses there. Service groups met there, as well as agency boards, neighborhood associations, ad hoc citizens. The downstairs librarian became a part-time booking agent. Traffic in and out of the library rose sharply, as did the number of people with library cards, book borrowing, and volunteer service given in return. All this paid off in dollar terms when it came time for the library to justify its budget to the Finance Committee.

* * *

When the library moved into its new building, people in town formed a human chain and respectfully moved each book by hand from stack to stack.

* * *

The Handel & Haydn Society persuaded the library to open late Sunday afternoons for concerts there — a fine place for a concert, sunlight streaming through the high-arched windows of the main reading room. Then as long as the place was open, why not Sunday hours before the concert, sherry and cheese after? A great hit, especially on winter days when it was really cold but you didn't want to stay buried inside.

From the Sunday concerts, it was a logical next step to Friday Night at the Movies; to midnight closings during exam week; to the Wednesday night town forums and the Monday night stack checks; and the special programs like the teen mime theatre in the Children's Room, the open play readings, the marionette circus, the sign-ups for charter bus excursions, the ceiling mural....

And the exhibits, the contests and prize competitions, ongoing through the year: the very short story contest, portraits of the future, remembrances of the past, $20-and-under photography, illuminated poetry, calligraphy, origami, baby pictures of local personalities, junk sculpture, holiday crafts, pulp novel trivia quizzes, literary evenings live from the Reference Room, wayside flowers, third grade nature study, drawings of the new recreation center. All entries displayed in the hallway area. Prizes, blue ribbons and mentions in the paper mostly, with a little corporate sponsorship here and there.

* * *

One of the contests solicits suggestions for improving life in the town. A record number of entries is submitted, stunning in its variety and creativity. The library staff, thinking of ways to keep enthusiasm going, decides on a suggestion mailbox, conspicuous but low-key. Every week the mail is cleaned out; the non-frivolous responses are posted, and (if the suggester has agreed) sent to those in charge.

Suggestions are also put on large index cards for filing, together with the name and address of the submitter (unless it's anonymous), and current disposition. Users of the file can write down their own comments on an idea, or write their own ideas (separate card), or contact the original responder. In this way, the library preserves a file of dreamers and dreams.

In a neighboring file are program ideas actually tried in practice. A library volunteer mails an annual solicitation to all clubs, groups, and organizations in the community, asking for one- or two-paragraph summaries of programs they've executed during the year, and some feedback on how they went, all this on a standard form. So the user here can get a sense of what fund-raiser met with what success, when was the last holly fair, what sorts of ideas have and haven't worked, and why or why not. There's a literature of tested programs inside, and staff have learned enough about them to help design one for you.

* * *

The Young Adult librarian, who will never forget the 300 letters he once sent out, runs a word-of-mouth résumé critique and job search service under his desk. He is ruthless and helpful. He also teaches and demonstrates eye contact, smiling, listening, and good posture.

* * *

A student calls in, looking for a passage in a Dickens novel, but no ride to the library today. The librarian pulls the book and starts to read: ''It was the best of times, it was the worst of times, it was the age of wisdom, it was the age of foolishness....''

*   *   *

The library goes undercover at the Octagon, the 8-screen cinema serving the tri-town area. First, loaning the theater space for early morning film showings. Then, sneaking in an evening art film under dubious pretenses, claiming faulty projection equipment, taking a calculated risk in film as ennobling experience. The public likes it enough to keep coming, as the theater gets leveraged into the culture business.

*   *   *

The reference librarian, poised at her desk, waiting for the phone to ring. AnswerWoman is her name. She is a walking, or rather a sitting reference library, for that is where she is stationed. She is trained to find facts fast, her track record being 90 percent of questions answered within three minutes.

In between calls, the librarian reviews new directories and edits the *Know Your Town* guide. She also updates her personal contact file, of people she can call upon with truly exotic requests. As far as books go, she can punch some numbers to see if a missing title is anywhere nearby, since all the libraries in the region have agreed to put their holdings on common computer tape. And if the title can be found, the library will secure it via courier-dispatched inter-library loan, which was pushed almost but not quite beyond its limits when one person called in for a 500-piece jigsaw puzzle with a Currier and Ives snow scene.

*   *   *

The Bookmobile tours the neighborhoods on schedule, bringing along the library bulletin and other news notes. The Bookmobile also makes home deliveries for people who are sick, disabled, or otherwise shut in. (High school volunteers handle some of this too.) If the corner pharmacy will deliver, or the local grocery, why not tax-supported institutions? Books are food (or drugs?) for the mind. If the homebound reader isn't sure what to choose, the delivery person will select some books from the caller's interest area and head out with a case full of wares.

*　　*　　*

All this activity assumes we will have a next generation of readers. The children's librarians see much of their job as getting kids to read, especially outside of school, especially during holidays and summer vacations, and to do this they have tried various temptations. But silver stars got boring. The deal with the trading card company couldn't be renewed. The Reading Olympics, the Book Trek, the Great Kids' Books and the visiting children's authors, the other campaigns keyed to popular culture all were okay, but packed only kid-sized wallops. Maybe the best incentives are really instilled by family and school. Do you have something to offer here?

*　　*　　*

The neighborhood contains libraries ranging from nebulous to surprising, and someone wants to know if people might be interested in publicizing their collections and maybe making discreet loans here and there within the group. A checklist appears shortly in the mail, where participants indicate that they are strong in Gothic horror and nonexistent in political science or vice versa. If there's time, a complete list of titles can be circulated and kept current. If not, the summary statement will still elicit a call or two. Either way, seeds for the neighborhood reading club will have been sown.

*　　*　　*

The Al Fresco branch library is open for business — Mr. Fresco being kind enough to donate this nice weather we're having. There's the crowd of regulars, and passersby wandering off the main street into an open courtyard.

Actually, the open-air library isn't a public library program at all, though its staff was involved in the planning. After debating how it should be funded, the library decided to pass this one on to local entrepreneurs, looking for right livelihood, and for creation of social and educational value.

In the courtyard, books are for rent: the proprietors buy hardcover bestsellers and editors' choices fresh from the market. Readers can pick today's papers off the rack, or sit on directors chairs leafing through magazines. There's a nominal sitting charge by the quarter hour, nickels and dimes, though no one gets hung up about it.

Such a popular gathering place has the outdoor library become that other branches have opened up. And it's seemed only natural to serve light refreshments. So cafe society has taken hold, a mile and a half from the interstate.

* * * * *

*

* * *

*

Here's How You Can Cook Up Community Ideas
of Your Own

(Just follow these easy step-by-step directions...)

Step One	Step Two:	Step Three
	Select one	
Select one	ingredient	Select one
ingredient	from Column B	ingredient
from Column A	(the type of	from Column C
(the giver):	program):	(the receiver):
— — — — —	— — — — —	— — — — —
Working mothers	Information	Preschool children
Teenagers	Training	Terminally ill
Veterans	Companionship	Neighborhood group
Experienced parents	Entertainment	Students over 40
Senior citizens	Special Skills	Displaced families
Divorced fathers	(sharing, &/or	Newly unemployed
Supermarket managers	dispensing)	Ex-convicts
Newcomers	Physical labor	Runaways
Volunteers	Employment	Complete strangers
Anybody	Space (meeting,	All comers
	&/or social)	(...or labels from
	Material goods	Column A)
	Recreation	

Example: Seniors (A) share companionship (B) with Runaways (C).
   See how far down you can extend the columns.
   How many other examples can you make up?

Step Four: Choose time values for operation.
(e.g., how many sessions, how long per session, total length of time)

Step Five: Pick a location, from the many available.

Step Six: Add flavorings to taste.
(sponsorship, cost factors, special conditions, etc.)

Step Seven: Heat A (Step One) until thoroughly warmed.
Mix with B (Step Two).
Fold A and B into C (Step Three). (Go slowly.)
Blend remaining ingredients. Simmer until tender.

The chef is encouraged to test new combinations! What other recipes would you like to try?

*

*   *   *

*

parks

It's a pleasure to walk where you're going along the linear park. And what a nice idea to build a park way winding from one end of town to the other. The park has become a boulevard. People, gearing down, have more time for mutual admiration.

*   *   *

The state Department of Forestry stops by to give advice about tree planting and care. They know about park design, too. Anyone can become a deputy park ranger by passing a short course and getting a certificate. This means you can go out and prune trees, or plant them in approved locations and become their legal guardians. Or you can care for a standing tree by adding your name to the wait list at the registry.

Topiary graces the park. Trees shaped by the resident pruners in the form of eagles, lions, children playing. One block is known as the Street of Owls.

Fruit and nut trees are planted by the park way. Berry bushes screen out traffic. Ladders and buckets are in the park shed. The edible landscape supplies quiet and shade, a place to rest, and a bountiful harvest.

*   *   *

You can't put *anything* on park land without the express written permission of the parks officials. Sentiment is strong for preserving pure green space against any infringement whatsoever. Policy is also that when something is built, the builder is responsible for matching park land elsewhere in the community. The ratio of green space to total area must remain constant.

Most neighborhoods have their own park policy and park commissioners to enforce it. Where parks are few, they make their own. Often they start with vacant lots. Find out who the owner is; serve notice of intent to beautify; make arrangements to spruce it up; think about what to put inside:

> Bird feeders
> Barbecue pits
> African violets
> A rock garden
> Lawn chairs for sunbathing
> A free-form bench or two.

* * *

Industries place scrap materials with play use potential in specially-marked containers. The playground crews come by once a week and take what they want. Many workers are parents anyway, thus strengthening the industrial-park connection. So on Saturday mornings for a while, construction is in progress.

The playground is built along a block of the linear park, full of the strangest and safest shapes and sizes that local architects and pediatricians could devise. When the playground opens, young children cry; they'll need a while to figure out what to do. To play anywhere inside is an adventure, which gives the playground its name.

Other playgrounds have themes — witch's castle, sky fortress, caveman's grotto, and (in the lake) castaway's island. Aphrodite's playground, which is one of the most popular, is sometimes adults-only during evening hours.

* * *

Inside another playground is a giant sandbox with fine white sand, inviting almost as a day at the beach. Adults play in it too, edging children aside. In winter, the sandbox moves into a vacant storefront. Twenty-four inches are piled on the floor. People shake the snow off their coats and pay a dollar an hour to dig in the sand. In the evening, therapy groups are held.

*   *   *

On his next visit, the forest warden remarks, "You know, you could have a town forest if you wanted. I mean real woods, where people could walk and feel nature close by. Where your executives could hang out during lunch, and songbirds could sing. You have that empty stretch of land by the edge of town, and you have kids at the voke school looking for field work credit. We could help you develop the land, and maybe also give you a shared greenbelt with the next town over. Think about it; we can talk more next time."

*   *   *

The self-appointed town naturalist lives in the town forest most weekends, showing her home to people she meets. There's hardly a person left by now who can't identify every tree and recite her ecological chains. Children take outdoor nature study, often using the self-guided trails. Each child learns to be a life preserver.

*   *   *   *   *

recreation

The jogging course at the airport (blue stripe on the floor) takes in all the departure gates from Northwest to Eastern. Finish with a workout at the airport gym. Locker and shower combinations, towel included, only a dollar. Catch your plane relaxed and refreshed.

At the bus terminal, an exercise class. The baggage clerk doubling as coach. Purses and briefcases at your feet. Pickpockets, get out. Ready, now — stretch, two, three, four. Now you can nap on your way home.

*   *   *

Most of the time we're first in line for a play street permit. It's our street, after all. We play the standard street games and the sports-pages sports. Basketball on the court we hot-topped ourselves. Living chess with 32 live pieces. But everyone comes onto the street to play volleyball. That's about 30 on a team, no side or end lines, and unlimited hits. Sometimes two volleyballs at once.

Then, once a year, the multi-street olympics, a full-weekend event, with opening games ceremony, an olympic runner with torch, uniforms, flags, anthems, medals. Giant games of dodgeball and cops and robbers. Fire escape climbing. Long-distance marbles. Hopscotch for the little kids. Plus the traditional pentathlon of boxball, stoopball, Chinese handball, stickball hitting, and running bases.

*   *   *

The Sunday morning softball game is an institution. First 18 on the field play. Some sleep in their cars the night before. Starting time edges gradually toward dawn.

From the pickup game, the neighborhood league, spontaneously combusting. Informal becomes formal, ditto becomes mimeograph, traditions rules, and scorecards ledgers. Fans gather to watch the Broadway Basenjis take on the Park Circle Pandas. The Sunday morning game, though, goes on.

The neighborhood league goes city wide. Neighborhood champions vie against each other, hard play, serious stuff. There is pre-game publicity and word of mouth, posters and general hubbub. The manager, amplified, drives his team through the streets in an open truck and rallies the masses.

The city championship is starred on the calendar. Cable TV is on the scene. The mayor throws out the first ball. Little kids will remember their parents and some grandparents in uniform. There is cheering, excitement, and aluminum chairs. Americana is sold in the aisles.

Neighborhood pride grows. The neighborhood fabric tightens. Memories will keep it tight for a while. Meantime, the football season is coming up.

*   *   *

Because the scale of the community is smaller, recreational events are often shorter. Concerts, for example, may take just an hour. Plays are frequently one-acts. There's no need to drag out an event simply because people had to pay a lot of money to attend it or travel a long distance to get there.

*   *   *

Because the community fits human rhythm, quiet periods are built in. It's no disgrace to rest in the middle of the day; if anything, the opposite.

Off the streets of the city you can find quiet rooms with quilted mats. The black shades with the moon and star designs are pulled down. Earphones with rolling surf if you like. Time for a short nap. You can leave wakeup instructions, or borrow a silent alarm as you walk in. Relax your whole body; breathe in deeply. Most of the sleepers will be wider awake later on.

The neighborhood is trying out tropical hours. Open in the morning, two- or three-hour siesta breaks, open again at three or four. How lovely to rest in the middle of the day and have late dinners. Evening hours are also good for business.

> *When hungry, eat.*
> *When tired, sleep.*
>   — Zen saying

*　　　*　　　*

The Rec Department is bulging with after-school and evening programs. They aim for all ages and as many sports as possible. They'll key programs to special target groups, like preschoolers, retarded, those in nursing homes. It's taking requests that stretches their limits; but you name it, and if we can get enough people interested in it we'll try it, and if it doesn't work maybe we'll go out and create the interest ourselves.

The Rec Department runs coaching clinics for teens; gym classes for infants; scuba diving for the physically challenged; skateboard rodeos; and multi-generational competitions, featuring the three-generation relay and the mother-son pairs.

They've begun to emphasize family recreation, where families can get together to play with each other or with or against other families as the case may be. Friday nights the gym is reserved for family groups. Late Saturday afternoon is for Family Feud.

*　　　*　　　*

The gallery is asked to quiet down before the start of the town poker championship....

*　　　*　　　*

The Rec Department office has a diligently-acquired game library, catalogued, with donations accepted, and a two-week checkout with recreation card. It keeps a file of game rules, plus suggestions for improvising equipment. It sponsors new games and hybrid games and ancient games and international games and made-up games which as far as is known aren't played anywhere else.

New games especially are played at the schools. The idea is to teach attitude toward sport, social values, inner games, as well as the outer game and the conditioning behind it. In Phys Ed, the roles of competition and cooperation are explored. During recess, the kids invent newer games, trusting their own imaginations. One class collects them, codifies the rules, consults a patent lawyer; the collection will be printed and sold, the proceeds used to keep the school from closing.

*   *   *

The Rec Department building is where most quiet games are played. A different game featured every night of the week: scrabble, bingo, checkers, computer chess, ping-pong. Weekends are open, but usually with an advertised special so that partisans will know to show up.

The staff also works on coping skills, and problem-solving skills, for re-creation is defined broadly. So troublesome games, as well as easy, are stocked and sponsored. Simulation games, like Outdoor Survival. Message games, like Global Hunger. A well-graded puzzle collection. Stumpers and Teasers. Combination programs, like Think and Swim. Math teachers compile some number games, trying to stay a step or two ahead of the brightest, but not always successfully.

*   *   *

The microcomputer getaway weekends seem to be attracting mostly singles, but possibly for the wrong reasons.

The kids in our town tell the kids in the next town over that they'll meet them in a no-questions-barred game of College Bowl next Saturday noon on the town line. The college admissions office will send out scouts.

*   *   *

Chess and backgammon boards are etched into park tables so anyone can play. Town-owned canoes are beached by the river for any swimmer to use. Parallel bars mark bus stops. Sunday afternoon is open Dungeons and Dragons, which often distresses non-playing parents whose kids skip supper.

In its brochure, the Rec Department argues for exercising the whole person, at the partial expense of blood and guts. But privately, staff wonder where holistic recreation stops and the *übermensch* begins.

*   •   •

The cleared land would make an ideal ballfield if it weren't full of rocks. The counselors paint the rocks with yellow swatches; the next day is Gold Rush Day, where yellow is gold. The kids haul in ore to be weighed on the assayer's scale. The more gold, the more tickets good for rides at the upcoming camp carnival. One camper doesn't put this all together until ten years later.

*   •   •

The family sits around the kitchen table playing a cooperative board game. The idea is not to best your opponents or be the first one home, but rather to see how well you can work together for common goals. The payoff matrices are non-zero-sum. For example, the object of the game called Ethics is to make moral choices; everyone is supposed to help everyone else become wiser.

*   •   •

Buses leave from Central Square at dawn. Half the town is going camping. It's an annual event, spending a weekend together in the woods, on the cooperative vacation land not far away. Or even in the state park. You have to clear out of the place every once in a while.

*   •   •

On winter Sundays, the hoedown in the town hall gets people out. Dancers spill into the corridors when the meeting room overflows. Before the dance and after, kids followed by their parents or vice versa carve snow sculptures on the grounds behind. Snapshots are taken of the frozen gallery. White ribbons are awarded; cocoa is poured. Some families build igloos and camp out overnight.

On Snowperson Day, snow men and women welcome you to the block. Large snow spirits, sturdy and with knit caps, watch over each house.

     •   •   •

The midnight basketball game is almost under way. Competition for court time is intense, since many players will sacrifice spare change and circadian rhythms. The last players will greet the aerobic dancers at dawn.

The people will pay to have the fields lit at night. A coin-activated switch turns on the power. There is romance to bocce and horseshoes and high-jumping practice under the lights.

The gym and the fields are open as long as people want to use them. Their use, after hours, is self-supporting. Closing down is rare. People will spread their activities around the clock if their choices are do it at an odd hour, or wait in a long line, or don't do it at all. Even if facilities were not scarce, the community would still keep openness and multiple options, which go with its definition of freedom.

     •   •   •   •   •

blocks

Building blocks:

An extra shed becomes a busy warehouse. Stuff is stored there belonging to the block, that all block members can use. A washer and dryer. An electric typewriter. A photocopier. Good dishes for company. All owned in common by the block, loanable through the sign-out log.

The block's basement shop has the latest equipment. The block darkroom turns out professional prints. The garage next door has a hatchback wagon. When many share the cost, more goods can be purchased.

*   *   *

Any visitor is welcome in the block guest room, American or European plans. Home guest rooms newly freed are used for boarders, studios, playgroups, piece work, whatever.

In apartment buildings, the music room is usually a few doors down from the common dining area and the shared professional office.

In the condominium, ten percent of the monthly maintenance fee goes to purchase shared goods and services. Shall we buy a word processor this month, or a small sailboat, or sponsor some children from overseas? These discussions also bring people together and clarify their values.

Ditto for housing projects, where ten percent of the rent goes to the modernization fund. Half of that could buy a full-time cop.

*　　*　　*

Apartment dwellers belong to the block. The block relates to the longer street. The street is part of the larger neighborhood. The neighborhood lies in a bigger district, and so on. These classifications are nested. The community member has many reference groups, a layering of supports. But much of community life goes on, and many community dreams are fulfilled, at the block level.

*　　*　　*

All block members belong to the block club, automatically. Block officers are elected annually, including the representative to the neighborhood council. Throughout the year, monthly meetings and less formal subgroup meetings take care of block business, not that you have to go to any of them unless you are interested.

There are block parties, quiet ones for sitting around, and raunchy ones, where a hired band blasts away until someone complains.

There are complaints, handed in on 5x7 red or yellow cards to the block representative, who deals with them accordingly.

There are block outings, vacation trips together, joint bank accounts, barbecues and picnics, athletic teams and tournaments, garden days and casual nights, where two or more is company.

There are meetings with the research team, which feeds back useful data.

There's a block study group, where people read divergent opinions on social policy and meet to tangle with social issues of the day.

The flute, the guitar, the bass, and the saxophone get together an evening a week and when the weather is nice they play in the street and draw a small crowd.

A block patrol can be activated should the occasion warrant. The patrol is like a volunteer fire department — not needed most of the time. But every so often, when things get tense around the neighborhood, it helps to have some people on the streets till later at night.

The block parent is home most of the time, and the whole block and most of the neighborhood kids know him by name. The decal in the window is common through town. (In apartment buildings, the decal is by the door buzzer.) If there's trouble, if a child needs help, the child knows where to go. Should the block parent be out, there's a backup, and a note left on the door.

The block parent's home is now the block office. Delivery persons leave packages there. Block residents leave house keys. Strangers come to seek assistance. Messages are left, belongings dropped off, and groceries picked up. None of this was in the contract.

At the block's holiday party, each child on the street gives a gift to a blockmate and gets one back in return.

*   *   *

Peking: " 'The residents' committee,' Comrade Ho began, 'is a mass organization.... We take care of the life of the residents in this area. If, for example, a widow with no children becomes ill, we help her to find a doctor and help her to buy grain or perhaps coal. Or if both parents are at work and there is no one to look after the old people in the home, we help to look after them. We organize groups of children after school and on holidays and organize activities for them such as singing songs, reading books, physical activities, and cultural activities.' "

*   *   *

There's a village feeling on the block. Everyone knows everyone else, strengths and weaknesses; life moves in peaceful rhythm. The words sound nice: the block village. Can the block really change its frame of mind? The block clubs turn into village assemblies. The parish imports sheep for the lawn. The chimesmaster tolls the village bells.

*   *   *   *   *

employment

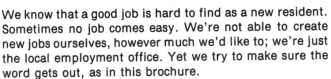

NICE WORK

AND HOW TO GET IT

We know that a good job is hard to find as a new resident. Sometimes no job comes easy. We're not able to create new jobs ourselves, however much we'd like to; we're just the local employment office. Yet we try to make sure the word gets out, as in this brochure.

Like any job hunter, you will probably be checking the standard sources: want ads, libraries, bulletin boards wherever you go; trade journals, agencies, family, friends, whoever you know. But in addition, the short list following mentions a few more places to look for jobs in our community. Perhaps you'll consider investigating these as well. And if you know of others, we hope you'll tell us about them!

Black books, and other tip sheets	These circulate mostly underground, and you're on your own if you buy their advice.
Career planning offices, in the colleges	Even if you're not presently a student.
Company bulletin boards, in particular.	If you can figure out a way to get in.
Headhunters	Sometimes visit on safari, and post public hours.
Hiring hall	Largely for day work, but not exclusively so. Non-union, as we co-sponsor it. Doors open at 6:00 a.m.

Home Business Monthly	That's our own newsletter; see also our courses for would-be entrepreneurs.
Job clubs	We can provide a complete listing.
Job fairs	We also run special job fairs for women, minorities, handicapped, autistic, prisoners, and so on. At the teen job fair, we usually bring a live band to get the kids out.
Job Match	Our local radio show.
Neighborhood associations and job exchanges	They often have listings which never reach us.
Supermarkets	Most have pretty good two-way notice boards.
Welcome Wagon listings	These also have company descriptions.
Worker cooperatives	Which often don't advertise publicly, and where barter arrangements if not jobs are likely to be available.

We'd also like to tell you about some of our other facilities and services, especially those not always found elsewhere:

§ Our job listings are mostly computer-filed, as well as in hard type. If you can't get our listings over cable, we'll let you sit by one of our screens; and if you're thinking of self-employment, you can look at the competition.

§ We run job-finding groups of most major kinds. Tell us whether you quit or were let go, whether you identify as blue- or white-collar, whether you are composed or terrified, and we can probably place you with others like yourself.

§ We also run groups in different formats. That is, some are practical and didactic; we teach you all the tricks we know. Others run more like Jobseekers Anonymous, where people stand up and testify. Those groups are more fervent, but we're still evaluating which work best. For both kinds, we train volunteer leaders so that we don't have to carry the whole load ourselves.

§ We check all clients to make sure they're getting all other services they need and are entitled to, and hook them up when necessary through our service broker, for we know that unemployment and other social problems go hand in hand.

§ We run workshops in applied persistence, beginning and advanced. You may see some of our graduates in the streets, carrying their own sandwich boards, passing out handbills advertising their availability, or otherwise acting shamelessly. We also teach "cold turkey" technique, walking right in on a prospective employer, and "wild turkey," camping out on the doorstep in certain cases, though we also warn that these strategies can backfire and lose power with collective use.

§ We have a special program for placing the mentally ill, current qualifiers welcome, for we have read that the costs of schizophrenia alone to the American economy run over $15 billion a year. Our sheltered workshops are usually full, but we presently do have some executive-level vacancies.

§ We have gotten together with local businesses and agreed on uniform voluntary quotas for hiring and then training women, minorities, and former convicts at both entry and managerial levels.

§ Finally, we have separate departments for different programs and people. Rent-a-Kid and Rent-a-Granny, certainly; job re-entrants and career-switchers, of course, We have a lively office pool for placing the most "hard core unemployed." Beyond these, one of our staff specializes in retraining human service workers; another handles the overqualified; while another works with computer programmers who have had it and want to go back to the humanities.

*   *   *

...Two, one, on the air...

Hi, my name is "Box 357," and I'd like to tell you a little about myself. I was a foreman over at the die works till it shut down. I was there for nine years, and know the machinery real well. I was pretty good with the men, too, and there are others who will speak to that. Right now I'm looking for the same kind of work or similar. You can tell by the color of my hair that I'm not just out of school. But if you're looking for a hard worker who is honest, quick to learn, and with plenty of good years left, please call the station and ask for me, 357. I was an independent trucker for a while also, so I'd have to say I'm pretty versatile. Thank you very much, and have a good evening.

*　　*　　*

Facing a three-hour layover, the traveler checks into Airport Temporaries. He can pick either volunteer or paid work or the special of the day. In basement offices, travelers stuff envelopes, handle light typing, solicit phone pledges, do some occasional consulting. Others mop the corridors or confirm reservations. Better to help someone or make a few bucks than to stare into space. The airport also keeps its costs down. Look, if 20 people offer two hours a day, that's a work week right there.

*　　*　　*

More people are changing jobs in mid-life or earlier. One lifetime career is no longer the norm. Some manage several careers simultaneously, by juggling their options. And those who pass through a sequence of careers are credited and honored. Fording streams ranks higher than drifting with the current.

> *Hey, young fellow, Navy has news for you*
> *If it's travel or service or pay you want,*
> *get into the Navy blue*
> *Navy trains you, gives you a job that's great*
> *Your rank will grow higher, and when you retire,*
> *you'll only be thirty-eight.*
>
> — old Navy recruiting jingle

The company has started its own inplacement service, for people who want lateral transfers.

"There should be a type of public insurance [educare] that would permit an individual, any time in his or her life, to receive financial support for x amount of time (usually no more than a year) to receive further education and training, regardless of practical utility. So, if a person wishes, say, to use the year to learn about archaeology, with no intention of becoming an archeologist, fine."

Career counseling flourishes. At the office, the client says:
"It's easier to change marriage partners than to change careers. But I can envision more than one quest. Why do I have to box myself in? Why do I have to diminish my identity?"
The counselor replies:
"I can understand your feelings. Career decisions are affirmations of mortality. So suppose you are right. What would you like to do about it?"

*   *   *

If you like your job, and maybe even if you don't, call up the employment office or school placement bureau and put your name and occupation in the career file. That way, people who are considering your line of work, new alumni or even strangers, can call you up and take a look around at what you do, ask you questions, and see how it feels for them. This prevents unhappiness. It's also a change of pace, especially since the last kid who came out asked some sharp questions and made a suggestion which wound up making your life easier.

*   *   *

Many more kids are in the labor force — they need both the money and the skill. Many more adults are interns, or apprentices — taking a chance, working at probationary wages, hoping to prove themselves.

And there's no formal retirement age. Most of those who want to keep right on working. Often they work part-time, or pick up a more casual job, or take another apprenticeship, or all three. The night manager at the 7-11 was 88 last month, knows how to handle herself too, won't stand for funny business.

*   *   *

Job tenure went out several years ago, about the same time as seniority. School teachers, college professors, and public employees in what used to be the civil service now work on contracts, one year at the beginning, three to five years for those who have earned them. At the end of the contract period, performance is reviewed, and reemployment is renegotiated. Retention and advancement are based on merit. Excellence is the primary patron.

*   *   *

As a new resident, you should know it's against the law here for pay differentials to be based on age or sex. Almost all of us believed in equal pay for equal work, so we did something about it. When we passed the law, many women's salaries and younger workers' salaries went up right away; others went up following appeal. This law cost money, which is why it didn't pass easily; a two percent tax surcharge was levied across the board to cover expenses, and will remain in place until adjustment costs are accounted for. But in this case, justice triumphed over the pocketbook.*

We've also just passed an ordinance limiting the highest municipal pay to 2½ times that of the lowest-paid municipal employee. The idea was that no one's labor was worth five or ten times that of someone else's — at least not on a base rate level — and that pay scales should be more equalized.

_____

*Our campaign slogan was "If we can't afford justice, what can we afford?"

This was a hard fight, and there may be a court challenge, possibly more than one, since some observers felt the measure didn't go far enough. There are bonus and incentive provisions, based on merit, which can stretch out or narrow the pay ratios slightly. (Merit funds are set aside in contract negotiations.) At any rate, our Position 2½, as some call it, is law only within local government. A few companies have been testing it out in the private sector, but the results are not yet in.

* * * * *

workplaces

Here are some reasons people like working at the company: It's not just the company day care center, or the rec room where you can leave your kids, or the nursing room for mothers, or the nurseries for babies.

It's not only the on-site gym or the discounts at the Family Y. It's not just the quiet room, soft furnishings and subdued lighting, where employees can come for realignment. And it goes beyond the interest group meetings, before and after work and at lunchtime, arranged through the activities coordinator. All these are fringes, no less but no more.

*   *   *

It's more that management by objectives is taken seriously, scrupulously even. Each employee sits down with his or her supervisor, once a year minimum, and works out a detailed employment contract with specific objectives, measurable objectives, jointly agreed upon.

Here's a contract sample, for a clerical worker:

PERFORMANCE CONTRACT

Name of Employee: Position Title:
Department: Start Date in Title:

Name of Supervisor: Position Title:
Date of Contract: Date of Review:

Item	Contracted Performance	Mutually Agreed On?	Actual Performance	Performance Rating
1. Attendance	Present 90% of work days	Yes		1 2 3 4 5
2. Promptness	Present 90% within 10 min. of start time	Yes		1 2 3 4 5
3. Phone manner-- pleasantness	80% rating by outside evaluator on dummy calls (minimum = 10)	Yes		1 2 3 4 5
4. Phone manner-- helpfulness		Yes		1 2 3 4 5
5. Typing	Min. 75 wpm, & max. 3 errors, by 3-minute test	Yes		1 2 3 4 5
6. Information	Score min. 80% on quiz on company matters	No		1 2 3 4 5
7. Reception-- complaints	Max. 2 in file/feedback box	Yes		1 2 3 4 5
8. Reception-- compliments	Min. 2 in file/feedback box	Yes		1 2 3 4 5
9. Appearance	Appropriate to office climate (Supervisor rating)	No		1 2 3 4 5
10. Attitude	Appropriate to position (Supervisor rating)	Yes		1 2 3 4 5
TOTAL RATING:	MEAN:			

[Actual performance and performance rating to be inserted. General rating guidelines follow:
1. Significantly above contracted standard (25%+)
2. Somewhat above contracted standard (10-25%)
3. At level of contracted standard (within 10%)
4. Somewhat below contracted standard (10%-25%)
5. Significantly below contracted standard (25%-)]

The overall idea is to sit down and meet shared goals and expectations, stated as clearly as the English language allows.

*   *   *

Job rotation, job sharing are ingrained in the system. Flexible hours and weeks are taken for granted. The home-work option and career insurance were thoughtful gestures. The Golden Rule plaque by the main gate adds a personal touch.

*   *   *

But incentive pay touches the heart of the matter. Employees get fixed base salaries, then graded bonuses depending on how well objectives are met. Measurable standards make performance assessment easier and fair. Wages are higher, but so is productivity. Union and management are pleased. When workers say they set their own pay, they are not entirely joking. Career ladders here have a rung of truth.

Whole programs are governed by goals and incentives, not just people. Each unit sets objectives and is accountable for them; so does the whole company. Criteria are set in advance, openly and mutually, and are closely followed by the outside evaluators. Divisional budgets are then based on works, not faith. The chief executive officer, explaining success, says company policy is to approach rationality.

*   *   *

Quality circles ring the factory. The job stress program tackles burnout and beyond. More workers are signing up for late retirement. The reduced summer hour elective is turning out well.

*   *   *

Some benefits are less conventional: If you are sick for a long time, you can draw from the sick bank. Staff can deposit up to half of earned sick leave there. If someone cannot work after sick days are used, a bank withdrawal can be made, on approval, from the fund of days that employees have left in common. Deposited days may also be cashed in upon retirement. An unemployment bank, based on similar principles, may be in the offing.

Courses at work are heavily enrolled, especially since the company gives scholarships and the community college needs the business. College credit is definitely available. One of the best-attended courses teaches how to be a more effective change agent inside, outside, or alongside the system.

Every seven years, workers can take a paid sabbatical, just like academics. Growth on the job is open to all. The company will match, up to half pay, wages left in the sabbatical fund. Or it will arrange placements in another branch, or in another non-competing company, even overseas, by consulting the industry job exchange. Exchange workers get premium pay, being fresh blood.

*   *   *

United States, 1942: Kurt Weill, the composer, organizes the "Lunchtime Follies," variety shows given at factories to improve productivity and morale and boost the war effort.

South Bend, Indiana: At the old Studebaker plant, workers turn out 200 hand-built Avantis per year, cost $27,000 per. Forget about punching clocks. Find your natural work rhythm and help yourself to refreshments. Bring your radio if it adds to your pleasure. Bring family and friends too; they can relax, or sit down next to you and pitch in.

Bolivar, Tennessee: The Harman plant makes rear-view mirrors. Workers go home once they've met their quotas, and don't look back.

Nearby, workers sign their products, adding home phones in case someone wants to call and chat about Quality. This has led to friendships.

*   *   *

The company has a Board of Directors which is representative of the community. Shareholders nominate, based on interest and ability. The Board assumes power over working conditions and activities at the plant. National firms have community boards, one per plant with similar powers, and with input into national policy decisions as well. One board, one vote.

The Board says let's share a holistic doctor to give advice on healthstyle. Let's bring in the health screening teams from the local hospitals. Let's ask the social service agencies to visit on-site, as part of their office hours. Let's have them train our staff in their techniques.

The Board says let's set up a Millfront Information Network as a collaborative project with other companies so that workers will have better access to community resources. We envision an office, a comfortable lounge, notice boards everywhere, visiting professionals, and an information coordinator who knows everyone's business inside and out. If our own company gets much larger, we might want a separate coordinator just for in-house R&D.

The Board says make inservice training a priority. All staff should complete so many hours a year, on topics approved by the training committee. Keep an eye on the best questioners. Develop intrapreneurs. Documentation should go in personnel files and be pulled in salary and promotion reviews. Do this for line workers and executives as well. In fact, new executives should get some training on the job before receiving full board certification, like at hospitals.

And let's call that consortium of local agencies and colleges and try their training and consultation services. They live here; they should know our needs. Their annual fee seems reasonable, and if they can deliver as promised — the skill-building programs, the problem-oriented site visits, the unlimited phone availability — we'll be getting help for cheaper than we could buy it from outside, and supporting our community's nonprofit sector too.

*   *   *

All of this only whets the appetite of those Board members who see profits as a necessary and desirable means to service. They press on:

•Upgrade our tours, encourage more of them, with kid and adult versions. Not just gloss and glitter, but real run-throughs, serious on-floor looks at what goes on, pointing out problems as well as assets. Let's find a rep to talk to school and community groups, not to proselytize, but to inform and provoke discussion; maybe someone who will evolve into a full-time community liaison.

•Use our corporate facilities after hours. We have all this space. Let the little tykes into the boardroom and show them what management is all about. Let them search the corridors for captains of industry. Let people in general have the run of the place during visiting hours and maybe with supervision on weekends, for this is good public relations.

•Open the company cafeteria to the public. Call up the restaurant reviewer and push it as a chic new place to be. Serve stylish cuisine, a wine list after five. Put up a small revolving stage with cabaret acts on Friday nights. Find a booking agent who will bring in bright new talent. Make sure the place breaks even.

* * *

The more activist faction supports these activities as far as they go, which they say is not very far. They argue that the company ought to move out more toward the community (its ultimate source of strength), not just pull the community in:

Release time is written right into the contract. As part of your job, you can elect to spend two percent of your work time in community service — volunteering for a local community agency, or engaging in some other approved betterment project of your choice. Some say two percent is nowhere near enough; maybe this can change.

You register your work with the community development director. Her department serves as a volunteer clearinghouse, in fact has a tie-in to the main clearinghouse downtown. She keeps records on participants and time, and also posts the volunteer opportunities which arrive daily.

What's more, the company has fanned the idea around the community, sparking other companies to start related programs of their own, with the middle-term goal of an integrated corporate volunteer network.

* * *

Staff signing up can also be part of a multi-company talent pool. When a special skill is needed, the right person is called. Technicians in particular shuttle around, are usually free to trouble-shoot next door, for it's one local economy. Time-shared executives are coming, right after Managers on Loan, but a little more groundwork must be laid.

* * *

The company has a contributions officer, to channel and assist in fund-raising efforts among staff. But the company also puts in dollars of its own, not just the sweat of its employees. Traditionally, ten percent of profits go to local causes. An in-house committee of randomly-asked volunteers, screened only for conflict of interest, votes on funding requests from outside. They enjoy giving company money away, or, more accurately, reinvesting it in the community. Their motto is the buck doesn't stop here.

* * *

The vice-president for operations, reminiscing, drifts back to her job interview. The Board had asked her how she'd improve working life. Her reply is still vivid:

"You remember Edward Bellamy's lines in *Looking Backward*, where he wrote:

> All trades shall be equally attractive to persons having natural tastes for them. This is done by making the hours of labor in different trades to differ according to their arduousness. The lighter trades, prosecuted under the most agreeable circumstances, have in this way the longest hours, while an arduous trade, such as mining, has very short hours....The principle is that no man's work ought to be, on the whole, harder for him than any other man's for him, the workers themselves to be the judges.

B. F. Skinner in *Walden Two* said much the same thing.

"My own views are quite similar. The problem is that translations from utopian fiction to real life have rarely been tried. Frankly, I think we've lacked the guts. But good management is always willing to experiment. If I come here, I want to put a labor-credit system into practice, more credit for jobs less desired. It will work, or we'll know why."

All this seems so long ago. Now, she wonders if she deserves all the credit-hours she's been getting.

* * * * *

The Pro Bono Talent Bank is open for business. Need a good lawyer, but can't afford to pay? Or an accountant, doctor, mechanic, therapist, guest speaker, or other professional service? Call the bank and see what's available. Many (not all) of the professionals in the bank make upwards of $50,000 a year. Why shouldn't they donate two, three, five, ten percent of their time? They should; and many do.

businesses

A couple of craftspersons in the community knew they needed more business, for as it was they were sinking fast. They wanted their own shop, but knew also that they lacked enough capital. So they sold shares; semi-publicly, to their friends and anyone else who would like a piece of the action. Ordinary folks bankrolled the store, just as angels finance a play or movie. No bank deals. No red tape.

Some risk, yes. But of course, having put in for shares, the investors had a stake in making the store work — i.e., shopping there, hunting for markets, spreading the word. They told the storekeepers: keep selling quality, price it reasonably, give yourself time, be your friendly selves, and let us do most of the worrying.

Success gets noticed. Similar ventures began springing up. A bakery, a fish market, a used toy emporium. More neighborhood businesses and neighborhood workplaces, launched by merchants without merchant genes, without expensive tastes, who wanted to make a living outside the large corporation but who couldn't do it any longer in public service. So they created public services of their own.

*   *   *

The storekeeper is an ally, a lookout, an anchoring point, a linchpin of the community support system. So is the store itself.

" 'If only we had a couple of stores on the street,' Mrs. Kostritsky laments. 'If only there were a grocery store or a drug store or a snack joint. Then the telephone calls and the warming up and the gathering could be done naturally in public, and then people would act more decent to each other because everybody would have a right to be here.' "

* * *

What the community bookstore lacked in mass-market discounts, it made up for in the tastefulness of its collection, the literacy of its clerks, the flavor of its coffee, and the bite of its conversation. Volunteer staff did get a 20% trade reduction and free admission to the Monday night story readings. The store was also the earliest place to get the Sunday papers, the latest place to close, and the only place to make home deliveries.

When you come into the tire store, there are light snacks while you wait, magazines to leaf through, toys for the kids, color TV turned down low. The floors have carpets and the windows have plants. It's like waiting in your living room, which is deliberate, for the owners want customers to feel at home.

Open house at the John Deere. Franks and beans by the checkout. Garden seeds for the ladies. Straight farm talk, and try out the new machinery. A few funny stories; the drawings later on. No one goes away without a cap.

* * *

Meanwhile, in the Deindustrial Revolution, fuel prices have made home businesses more competitive. Transportation and distribution costs are lower. Labor-intensive cottage industries make hand tools, clothing, furniture, steeping themselves in the skills that used to belong to the country. Less commuting eases the sting of slightly lower pay. Workers feel attached to the product of their labor and to the people they work with. Bonds of collective work tighten the community frame. Was this how it used to be?

.   .   .

The donut shop, as patron, displays the work of local artists. If it sells, the manager retains the right to pay off part in honey-glazed.

In the same vein, the pizza shop owner, whose back room is already a youth hangout, thinks about converting it into a Youth Center, capitalizing on what kids already like to do, namely, eat.

.   .   .

The new stereo owner is surprised at the call from the high fidelity store. "Hello, is this Timmy? This is John calling from Acme Hi-Fi. I wanted to ask how you were finding your new stereo. Is it working out all right? Any problems with it?...Okay, that's good.

"Listen, what I'd like to do is send you a little evaluation form in the mail. It helps us follow up on our services and think of ways we can do a better job. All you need to do is mark the boxes and add any comments you want, then send it back to us. Would you be able to do that?... Great. Oh, when we get the form you can pick a free album down at the store....

"Remember now, if anything comes up or there are any questions you have, just give me a call or come on down and I'll try to help. Thank you, too, Timmy. Bye for now."

The department store hands out forms at the doors. The supermarket asks "Can we check out your thinking?" The service station grabs you before you drive away. People are getting tired of having their opinions asked.

.   .   .

Annie's Country Kitchen moves out around nine. Dominick's Bar moves in the same time. Sharing the space is working out fine.

.   .   .

The Tough Times Cafe is of the community, not just in it. The community supports the bar; therefore, the bar supports the community. Its owners decide to turn a third of the profits toward community causes. One year it hosts a spectacular party, food and drink on the house. The following year it gives rebates. The next year it donates to a community charity. The year after that it makes matching grants and thinks of turning itself into an independent foundation.

Following the leadership of the bar, other businesses begin profit-sharing. The record shop donates records to the library. The vegetable stand gives to the food bank. The building supply puts up a park bench. The shoe store, tying in with the voter registration campaign, gives away sneakers to new registrants and tells them to vote with their feet.

The merchants meet later and decide on other private sector initiatives. They will give five percent of their profits this year toward the operation of the downtown shopping bus. Next time, maybe they'll find another cost-effective model. They're ready to profit-share with the town, trusting that the town is ready to profit-share with them.

*   *   *   *   *

arts

A metal sculpture stands one morning near a bus stop. A mural appears on a once-blank wall. A mobile hangs out from an office roof. The art vigilantes have struck again.

Sometimes their creations linger, sometimes they move, sometimes they disappear altogether. They are regulated by artistic license. The vigilante artist knows when his creation has outlived its social usefulness.

*   *   *

Early on Saturday, the painter packs her gear and walks to work. The palette symbol marks the artist's spot. She paints outside, while a small group assembles. They ask: she explains about composition, color, and texture. She talks between brushstrokes. She is, by acclamation, the artist in residence.

*   *   *

The state has a small but finite line-item budget for the arts, and uses part of it to sponsor visiting artists. They receive one-year fellowships to go round the state and teach. Artists apply, as do towns to receive them. If ten artists visit ten different towns for a month apiece, that's a hundred towns a year. Annual cost, maybe $250,000. A luxury?

Once an artist is assigned, individuals and groups sign up to learn from him. The artist is at the town's disposal. He lives there during the week, shows his stuff, ventures his opinions, hits the neighborhoods, mingles with the locals, cross-pollinates.

The artist says "Why stop at visitors like me? Why not cooks-in-residence, surgeons, philosophers, civil engineers? How can we justify keeping knowledge to ourselves?"

*   *   *

Neighborhood artists get together to buy their own gallery. It's collectively owned and run by an elected steering committee. There's space for all the visual arts — painting, photography, sculpture, multi-media. Members display their own works and organize special exhibits. They give talks, run classes, support each other's work. They sell direct. New shows are social events, with wine and cheese, beer and pretzels, and an invitation to the entire neighborhood.

At the nursing home gallery, profits go for client care. The walls attract visitors, who stay for lunch.

The gallery makes much of its money by selling to businesses. Alternatively, it will rent its holdings, or lease them, and turn them over every so often. It also arranges with wealthier businesses to commission new works, to bring gallery exhibits to corporate lobbies, and to add dignity and serenity to individual offices.

*   *   *

Art moves outdoors whenever possible. Art needs fresh air. When it's behind closed doors, even in public buildings, fewer people are likely to see it, or know it exists.

Construction walls are fair game for any budding or budded artist. And on the graffiti wall near the center of town, anyone can write or draw anything he likes. A city block of spray-painter's heaven. The work is thrilling. Every month it's photographed, painted over, and a new pattern emerges.

Once a year is clothesline day. Two long clotheslines stretch the full length of the main street. Art hangs on the line, flapping gently in the breeze. There are student, professional, and open divisions, and the judges are the voting public. On clothesline day, the street is flush with talk about beauty. Competition is intense for the coveted golden clothespin.

* * *

Reputedly in Maine: Two thousand school children head down to the square. It's Paint the Town Square Day. Each child has a one-yard section of pavement to work on. Choose your own media, your own design, or get together with your neighbor if you like. Two thousand artworks by sunset. You can't walk without stepping on art. After a while, when the paint wears away, they'll start over again.

* * *

New York: The artist leaves 500 Cinderella slippers for people to take home from the steps of the 42nd Street Public Library, because they deserve them.

* * *

The pianist is playing a Liszt etude in twilight on a summer evening. She is swept away by the sonority of the piece, the passion bursting from its notes. She fights a losing battle to keep her long hair off her face. The audience is transfixed. A street game stops.

She is playing atop a flatbed truck. Tomorrow night she will drive to a different part of town, and the scene will be repeated.

There's a noontime concert series by the plaza. Every day in warmer weather, someone is on stage. All styles: classics heavy and light; jazz rooted and free; some pop, some rock, some traffic, some babies. Local talent mostly, with open mike once a week.

January: A community sing in the auditorium. Slides on the screen with the words. Several hundred voices swell in unison; four generations of singers, and of songs. "Alexander's Ragtime Band." "Winter Wonderland." "Hey, Jude." Today's top hit. The singmaster plays a trumpet solo and blows the crowd away. Afterwards, hot cider, and gathering around the piano after that.

Boston, Mass.: The Paul Winter Consort in Copley Square on a Friday evening in July. A free concert outdoors, crowd maybe a thousand. They play "Wolf Eyes," whose theme comes from meeting up with wolves in the northern forests. German shepherds in the audience begin to howl. Paul Winter asks the audience to join in, to feel as wolves. A thousand people are howling downtown. A full moon rises over the John Hancock Building.

*　　*　　*

The subways and buses feature poems by local poets and prints by local artists, part of the Arts in Transit series. They will be trying country music and participatory skits. Proposals have come in for serialized novels and comic strips.

*　　*　　*

Who is that guy all dressed up in a blue costume moving through the streets telling fairy stories to anyone who will stop and listen?

*　　*　　*

Summertime is also time for movies off the walls. An ad hoc group pieces together a film series and shows it in the newly-whitewashed outdoor cinema and handball court.

Usually more than one film series is going on. One is sponsored by the library, another runs most of the year at a local pub. Neighborhood and block groups have taken to combining their videodisc holdings and making their own schedules, also taking advantage of inter-neighborhood loan.

Public television in town means television which is open to the public. One of those large-screen TV's in a once-abandoned school building is free to anyone who wants to watch. Regulars vote on the programming. Shy people sit next to each other to keep warm. It's okay to nod off at the late movie, stay the night.

In summer, the set moves to the esplanade outside. Suppertimes are semi-potluck. One man always brings a bucket of popcorn to share, and others make lemonade.

*　　*　　*

The local movie theater extends its range in response. It opens up for daytime meetings and conferences, for special films, for live events on stage. The lobby expands, with sofas, plants, happy hours, and filmworks in progress. A steering committee plans future showings, based on viewer feedback. Announcements precede the movie itself. Afterwards, those who'd like to discuss the film meet in the manager's office.

* * *

After the curtain falls on the play, cast and director come out to talk with the audience. What did they think? What about the portrayals, the stagecraft, the pacing, the overall impact? What are their suggestions? The stage manager takes notes. The notes are typed, distributed, studied, and taken to heart.

* * *

The P.A.L., having checked out the outdoor sculpture exhibition, is heading this week for a tour of the recording studio. We run this program, the Captain and founder of the Police Arts League says, because we feel that the arts are a civilizing and humanizing influence on all kids.

* * *

Pickup folk dancing in the park. The phonograph plays music of all nations. The mood is active and brisk, zestful and dignified. Traditional enjoyment, where all can join in, for heritage is open to anyone.

Dance Free Friday night. Pump all the poison from your system. The music is taped, a new tape made each week by one of the Dance Free Collective. All musical styles and paces. Dance with others; dance by the mirror; dance with your self. Drink orange juice. Join in a circle; snake through the room. Heat up, let yourself go. Find your dancing nature, and set it free.

* * *

Each neighborhood has a box office now, run by its own residents, operating usually from a booth or desk or beat-up table in the community center or other nearby location. Low overhead means it undersells Ticketron.

On the walls are charts of ticket availability, by section. The volunteer staffer can also tell you about unadvertised specials. And between selling tickets, giving information, and forming connections, he handles the publicity for neighborhood events, which route their tickets through the box office too.

*   *   *

The local museums and cultural institutions decide on a collaborative. Aiming for better use by school/community groups, and better attendance, they offer incentives. They open a competition on how those groups could use the collaborative's services. Winners get cultural vouchers, lines of credit; they get to contract with the institution they choose, then work out a program of their choice. That was how Van Gogh came to the South Side, and how the Hispanic cultural center got underway.

Many museums and auditoriums stay open after hours anyway for special community functions. They take a percentage of the gross. There's something a little extra about paintings at midnight, or public lectures at dawn, or your own holiday concert, or a Saturday morning ballet where you meet the performers at brunch.

*   *   *

Look, up in the sky...! The Sky Art project is testing new kite designs. Watch out for low-flying human-made objects. Nighttime is for laser lights and fireworks rehearsal, and the sky will blaze.

*   *   *

Skokie, Ill.: Fel-Pro, Inc., a gasket company, hires a sculptor-in-residence, figuring that the private sector has a responsibility to support the arts. They give him the salary of a mid-level supervisor, access to machines, full artistic freedom, and no time schedules.

Copper and rubber sculptures perch in the lobby and gaze over the parking lot. They hang on the walls, lurk in the stairways, and guard the factory floor. His work is admired; it's given as prizes. Production workers, looking at the sculptures around the plant, begin to tinker with new ways of putting materials together....

*   *   *   *   *

beautification

Today is green-up and clean-up day. We're going to sweep the streets and wash the walks. We're going to plant trees and flowers and anything else with leaves. We're going to make things shine and get ourselves exhausted. Then we're going to party.

We'll pull weeds at the park, and scoop scum from the river. The bird feeders need a cleaning, and the fish pond should be restocked. Pull the tar roller over this way. When's the dedication of the new herb garden? Watch out for that sandblasting machine! Send that preschool crew over here next.

We're going to patch the small cracks, and press the city on the big ones. Those fire hydrants could use a paint job, maybe naval heroes. Personal touches on the lampposts should be okay within limits. Will totemic pole carvings get in the linemen's way?

*   *   *

A plant-lover on the block buys a bunch of window boxes wholesale and sells them to neighbors at cost. The block has the greatest profusion of flowers per capita for miles around. They are dazzling; symbols of hope in the world. On a more practical level, they fight crime, for somehow it's harder to break and enter when a petunia is looking you in the eye.

Bloomsday is declared; other outlets are sought; one corner seems like a good spot for a community flower bed.

Boy and Girl Scouts spread beauty further. (They're working together on a joint project.) Flower sales to corporations count for half their profits. It looks like they'll be flying to the worldwide jamboree.

.   .   .

Every so often, the Natural Resources Department has some extra plantings. The notice in the paper asks people to drop by and pick them up. You're also welcome to visit anytime and see what's on hand.

The senior class gift is a grove of trees, in a park close by the center. Their roots give wisdom; other classes follow them.

The landscaping at the shopping mall, the English garden especially, was more an economic than an aesthetic decision, but the plants can't tell the difference, and neither can most of the customers.

Where are all these plants coming from? Many of them come from a nursery run by the association for the retarded. It's a kind of sheltered workshop. The workers get background in successful nurturance. The plants are sheltered as well. Everyone is excited to see things grow. Prices are usually below retail; and oxygen is added to the air.

.   .   .

The Green Guerillas are in league with the local nurseries. They walk in unchecked looking for whatever they can get. They walk out unstopped carrying sacks of soil or seeds in their pockets, and sometimes actual plants or shrubs which they low-bridge out the door. At night, they strike where the earth waits expectantly, calling up later to claim responsibility.

.   .   .

Trees along the street are up for adoption. You can put your name on a waiting list and take a parenting course. (No stigma attaches to being single, since many school kids have signed on.) When adoption becomes final, it's your job to care for your tree, to water and fertilize it, check for illness, prune when necessary, and watch it grow. If you want, you can put a very small sign up near the base. Adoptive parents meet occasionally with the tree-planting memorialists and swap notes; together, they've drawn up tree maps for distribution.

If you don't want to adopt a tree, you can adopt a rock — a big rock that is, a permanent fixture. Not everyone knows that rocks are much happier when they are kept clean of markings, picked free of glass, and weeded from time to time. Anyone can adopt a tree, but it takes a special person to adopt a rock.

.   .   .

Beauty is sound as well as sight, natural sound especially. There's agreement in the neighborhood to be mindful of introducing new sounds, both quality and level, and both in relation to time of day. This doesn't preclude street music or power saws; yet as much as people value community around here, they also value peace and quiet. Simple respect, mostly, though the orientation packet spells this out in a little more detail.

.   .   .

Not too far from a school for the blind there's a fragrance garden, with flowers set off by smell. Follow the signs in English or Braille. Inhale deeply.

.   .   .

Tonight the neighborhood is dressed for the ball. Its sidewalks have been bathed and scrubbed, its benches freshly painted. All day long the neighborhood has been planted and raked, brushed and sprayed, combed and rolled. Now gas lamps are ignited, the lampposts beribboned; pennants wave gently in the breeze. Everyone gets ready for the group picture.

So what? Who cares? Take your ribbons and choke. Take your Barbie-doll dream and shove it. The world outside is rotting to the core, and you speak of perfumes, which only mask the stink. No more circuses; give us daily bread.

*　　　*　　　*

The neighborhood's glow tonight is only skin deep. Beauty can hide the truth; beauty alone won't save us. Yet in defense of beauty, outer beauty too, note that it is reinforcing. It makes us look again, return to its source. Beauty is restorative. Beauty in the community bonds people together; it's a force for stability. And since beauty is fragile, we want to protect it. It feeds our spirit of devotion, adding purpose to our lives.

*　　　*　　　*　　　*　　　*

families

Community starts with family, the first leap outside the self.

* * *

Many parents take a childbirth course at the local hospital. The methods of childbearing are described, the usual exercises are suggested, so are ways parents can help each other at birth. But what does it mean to issue a life? How do you want your child to grow? Where should instruction start and stop? The couples so challenged support each other, are catalysts and foils. Several become friends.

Just before delivery, the teacher passes out a list of experienced parents in the area who are willing to answer questions, give advice and possibly come over to lend a hand. A Big Sister (or Brother) program, adult version. Later on, you can go on the list yourself, taking a slight pediatrician's discount as an incentive. This is a joint obstetric-pediatric service; the doctors, who believe in quality of life after birth, thus fulfill a commitment.

* * *

Pierre the Pelican swoops into the maternity ward. Pierre is a newsletter on parenting, free for the asking. (The Mental Health Association at work.) He offers tips on childraising, friendly reassurance, survival stories, local parent news. He will also visit you at home, but being more modern than the stork, prefers to use the mail.

*　　　*　　　*

Shortly after leaving the hospital, new parents receive another list — this time with preschool playgroups, goods exchanges, babysitting co-ops, children's resources in general. The seeds of cooperation are planted. Later on, there'll be a reunion for the childbirth class. And in a while, a toddler parent will call. The Toddler League needs to perpetuate itself.

These programs are pushed most heavily in the poorest parts of town. And especially toward single teen-age mothers-to-be, who are high-risk and usually know it. The clinic runs a special group for them which meets once a week for warmth and contact, and for discussions of child care, nutrition, exercise, getting out, dating, jobs, and future plans. Many groups keep meeting after their babies are born. Each premature parent is also linked with a buddy, someone who's been through it, as an added source of support and sometimes of hand-me-down clothing.

*　　　*　　　*

The Welcome Baby Wagon showers the new arrival on the block with creative playthings.

*　　　*　　　*

Parent education is easy to come by. Parenting columns in the newspapers. Reader forums, advice swaps. Parent Reflectiveness Training. "How Would You Handle It?" on the tube.

Parents are supported, through targeted groups which serve (here's a sample) first-time parents, mothers over 40, instant parents (those newly married to spouses with children), and grandparents, at home and away.

And parents have room to grow, through their support networks and through associations like Parent-Child Encounter,

Parents in Action (films and live demonstrations), and the Parental Values Institute, which is dedicated to moral superiority.

*   *   *

Go to the marriage mediator if you want to. Pick up a copy of the trouble-shooting guide. Or if you like more structure, try the marriage arbitrator. There you have to co-sign agreements in advance, though you can pick non-, semi-, or full-binding forms. All this is a branch of the local district court, or family counseling center, depending on jurisdiction.

Wedding anniversaries are listed in the paper. The married couple is treated with respect. Friends and relatives bring presents to their door. Some hold food; others throw rice. One is for nourishment, the other for renewal.

*   *   *

Most kids grow up in extended families, as older parents move in with their children. The kids themselves less often fly the coop. Housing costs are higher, so is the cost of living, and fewer are living alone. The mother and father get child-raising help from extended family members. The kids get the advantages of multiple role models and being counted upon.

Grandfather and granddaughter walk to the store to pick up groceries. Granddaughter reads aloud to grandfather, whose sight is poor. Grandfather teaches some songs, and reminds about chores. They spend the day baking apple pies together. This is not a fairy story.

For kids growing up in group houses, it can be the same way. In these houses, the "home body" is a designated adult who stays home during the day and attends to children's needs. This person can be a natural parent, or not; the job can rotate, or not; and more than one body is often around.

The multi-generational group houses are modern extended families, with varied familial styles. They advertise themselves accordingly. From the group house catalog, you can select strict or lenient discipline, bounded or free feeling, high-, medium-, or low household responsibility, as you wish. If you don't love your present family, you can choose another when your lease is up.

*   *   *

If the block is close, there are block eyes on the street. People know the neighborhood kids and watch over them. Children feel adults even at a distance. More often than not, their spell is positive.

Godparenting is also in fashion; a child may have a dozen. Little ceremonies are common. Some block members, out of duty or boredom, become godparents to all kids on the street. Others act the same way, without need for the trappings.

*   *   *

Parenting is stressful, and it's easy to unload on your children. (Let's also not forget vice versa.) Where reports of child abuse or neglect have been verified, parents are required to enroll in an instructional group. It's like remedial teaching, extra help. Group members learn stress management techniques, how to deal with anger, and specific parenting alternatives; they practice them in class. This helps a little: so do the homework exercises, the follow-up sessions, and especially the company of peers. Sometimes the combined techniques turn things around.

But prevention is better. The Family Hearing Center specializes in parent-child disputes. They listen hard twice; they're good at unraveling, explaining, and calming people down. Binding arbitration is not employed here.

The parent stress hotline is another safety valve; and it's good there are other people to leave the kids with for a short time and be by yourself. Or if you'd like to leave, check the roster of Families on Call — they'll take you in for a while.

Sometimes it's the kid who needs to get away. In this case, Pinch-Hit Parents, neither friends nor relations, will step in for up to a few months if the child can't live at home. They are carefully selected and trained; usually the child's family pays for room and board. This vacation period often sorts problems out. When it doesn't, the Share-a-Family program offers more permanent placements.

*   *   *

When informal family structures are weak, formal ones give them a boost. The community center, parent division, has weekly events for parents and toddlers. There's "Dad and Me" for fathers and daughters; "Mom and Me" for mothers and sons. Family swims at the youth club. Family gym at the college. Family beat-the-blahs days on winter weekends. Family games and tournaments, where each family plays as one.

Kids out of diapers visit parents on the job, after school and on vacations. This meets multiple needs. Some are little bosses, T-shirts and all. Many want to work, not hang around; the company puts them on the fast track.

Parent-child award nights at the high school. Child-parent award nights at work. Family church days on Sundays. Family sections in the newspaper calendar. Movies rated F for Family, with family admission prices.

Gradually, informal structures grow stronger. That can be expected; family life is rewarding. The family hugs, the just sitting around together; the twilight walks, the clean-up days, the holding hands at meals; the strict observance of the Children's Hour; the sharing of dreams. This is good sentiment, as well as sense. When times are tougher, we move closer to the core. Family life becomes harder, denser, more satisfying, more prominent in the terrain.

*   *   *

Left and Right wings join hands at the rally. Hoist the same banners: "We're for the Family." They find they agree on values in principle. Most of the community appears to be there, not all that surprising; the pro-family majority is the whole population.

*   *   *   *   *

traditions

There is a prayer meeting in the home, with singing and holding of hands. Neighbors feel the holy spirit reach down and lift them up.

Many people around the block have started to eat Sunday meals together, to talk informally, have a drink or two, let the kids play. A time also to review the events of the week, do some business, plan something new, and enjoy each other's company.

On Easter morning, the group climbs to the top of the highest mountain and prays for the rebirth of their souls.

*   *   *

The graduating class throws a party for their parents every year. Mothers and fathers, guests of honor, are thanked for their help and support. It's a bittersweet occasion — a celebration of accomplishment, and a shared acknowledgement of growing older. For many, the nest now empties. Intergenerational couples crowd the dance floor. Flowers rest in multi-colored hair. Tears are exchanged for boarding passes. Everyone is flying to the next stage of life.

*   *   *

One month past the Fourth of July is Interdependence Day, when we celebrate our connectedness, declare the need we have for each other to make our lives whole. How many interconnections can we form? (Naturally, we dramatize this out of doors.) The entire group comes together for merrymaking and reaffirmation.

* * *

There are community rituals. The town-wide holiday honoring the birth of its patriot. The blasts of the whistle at noon and at sunset. Walking down the street of jack-o'-lanterns at Halloween. Recitation of the town legends to the freshman class. New rituals are conceived and incubated, tested for poignancy. The saturation point has not yet been reached.

The town photographer captures the highlights of the year and places them in the community scrapbook. Some of the shots are the same each time, for the historical record.

On Valentine's Day, the banks are closed.

On Founders Day, residents dress up in period costumes and enact the day as if they were living 100 years ago. If only Founders Week, Founders Month were feasible....

* * *

Local history is taught from third grade up, again in junior high. This develops identification with the community, and pride. One fall, the junior high students create a historical calendar with notes about people and places of yesterday.

Their research sheds light on some poorly understood events, while uncovering new ones. Using their teacher's help, they get the calendar professionally printed, then sell it around town to raise money for the historical society.

With the money raised, and together with the society and the Art Department, the sophomore class designs and installs historical markers for two dozen community sites. Youth crime decreases.

* * *

At Thanksgiving, the inter-church office serves as a connecting point for people who will be alone on the holiday, and helps them find each other and form temporary families for giving thanks together.

One Thanksgiving night each month, another family celebrates its good fortune with a meal of rice, tea, and fruit, and gives the money saved to UNICEF.

* * *

The retired couple invites everyone over to their house for Christmas dinner. They send a letter to the newspaper with an invitation open to one and all, pauper or millionaire, the only condition being that you would otherwise be alone on Christmas Day. Peace and good will are meant for strangers. Just call ahead to let them know you are coming.

* * *

On Christmas Night, the community sings outside. Before the sing, carolers roam the neighborhoods. Neighbors leave their houses to join them, or offer them refreshment. In the center of the square, beneath the stars, the town sings "Amazing Grace."

* * * * *

afterword

The search for the ideal community must not be abandoned. The belief that shrinkage is inevitable is self-fulfilling. If our mindsets go sour, if we accept the agenda of slash and burn, we hold a ticket to desolation.

When the battle is being fought between those who would cut back services and scuttle community and let the chips fall where they may, and those who count themselves "progressives" for shoring up the same doddering system one more year, then those of us who care about our own communities may legitimately look for another battlefield. We can say your agenda is not mine, your options are not mine, and we will find new options of our own.

There is no one way, but there are many ways. There is the way of organizing within the current system. There is the way of sneak inside attacks. There is the way of systemic confrontation, this with multiple hues. There is the way of charity, for those who can afford it. There is the way of self-transformation, for those who can afford that. There is the way of preventing nuclear war, so that some ways will be viable. There is the way of alongside, of feeding off the resources of the present system, until your system grows strong. There is the way of attempting life free from the system altogether, though that's hard to do.

Community Dreams is a way. Its way focuses on tinkering with the equipment, on altering the mindset with which we see our communities. It offers options, partial visions, on approval, for review.

This way assumes that we want to be powerful and to control our own lives. It assumes that as governments cut back, our home communities and neighborhoods will become more important — more needs will be met there. It assumes that we will have to take more responsibility for our home communities. And it infers that we are most likely to find power and control, and gladness and joy, closest to where we live.

Community Dreams is a collection of small-scale, local-level ideas which can be set into motion in most communities by yourself and the people you know. There are exceptions. But generally speaking, the ideas here can be implemented with relatively little money, technical expertise, physical equipment, government intervention, or time. They rely instead on cooperation, trust, openness, sharing, and strength of will.

Some of the dreams related here are fictional — really dreams as far as I know. Others are factual, based on personal experience, or on what people have told me, or what I've read about. Others are hybrids, centaurs, and mermaids. The boundary lines between fact and fantasy are blurry, which makes little difference in this case, for this is not Scholarship, and the truth-value of these dreams is not at issue. What's at issue is sparkle. And especially at issue is convertability, practicality, for *Community Dreams* is meant to be a book of practical utopias.

Some dreams mentioned may seem tame to you. Others may hover at the edge. But mainstream to one is margin to another; our experiences, like our communities, are not complete nor uniform. So we need deeper channels for importing ideas. We need more idea markets and more shipping lanes. We must broaden the horizons, lower the barriers, find new ways for making connections and for looking at our communities with fresh eyes. Fantasies, guided explorations, extended dream voyages can help us do this.

Nondreamers reply:
We already have it.

                                          Then don't take it.

We don't need it.

                                          Then don't use it.

We can't do it.

                                          Maybe. Maybe not.

It's a poor idea.

                                          That's quite possible.

236

It won't work.

Maybe you could modify
the idea for your own
setting.

*We have too much
to do already.
[Leave us alone.]*

What are you doing?
or
Save it for another time.

It's a Band-Aid.

You are cut and bleeding.

The point is not that every single dream can or should find its way into your own community. We respect won'ts, can'ts, and yes-buts. But figure two, three, five percent slip past the censor and into the big dream theater. Figure you match five percent with five of your own. Figure that a few make it onto the real life playing field. If you as reader were to take a *single* idea from this book or from your imagination and put it into operation where you live, that could be magnificent. The goal for you as dreamer is to seek the right dreams for yourself, free some more of your own, find your moment, and make your move.

I can hear another objection, cutting deeper this time. The most elegant street life, for example, the most spectacular festivals, the most careful attention to personal or communal beauty will not stop thievery, or end social brutality, or find people jobs, or housing, or raise people's incomes, or improve public health in as yet proven ways. One may argue (though misleadingly I think) that these first-named preoccupations, which we have embraced, are more frequently associated with lives of poverty and desperation. We are then advocating Band-Aids at best, bonbons at worst, in a society crumbling at the center.

Yet I believe this is not so much an objection to dreamwork as a statement about social structure and its resistance to change. Tear-stained limits bound any intervention. Reformers will meet their wailing wall. Most interventions fail, or fade away fast. Only a handful yield enduring and desired change; only a thimbleful change which is also widespread. It is hard, rock-bottom hard, to leave a lasting mark on one's community, much less society. And so it may be wise to honor any actor, simply for acting, apart from goals and technique. Those can be more easily taught.

Still, the fact is we need more community dreamers and more community dreams. When others talk of shrinkage, we must be countercyclical and talk of utopia. We must talk utopia to those we meet and those we teach. We must train new generations of utopians to rise in our places.

Utopia has a bad name in our society, a sign of the times. Utopians, they are foolish, and also vaguely dangerous. Yet would you not live in the utopia of your choice? And if you would, will you then blot it from your mind? How much less will you settle for? Are you willing to take one step, or another?

Steps must be taken, for dreams alone will get us noplace. At some point, community dreams must be converted to reality. The mechanics of conversion are not for this book, belonging rather to the literature of community organization, written down and yet to come. Conversion will take skill; but however much skill may be needed, the drive to get going must be no less strong. Skill must be accompanied by will. Skill training must be accompanied by behavior modification of the spirit.

To modify means to look for inspiration. Inspiration is your option-maker, your dream generator. Inspiration should be treasured wherever it is found, and it is found in silence and in conversation and in falling leaves for one ready to receive it. May we be ready, and ready to share it and fan its flame.

A few years ago, on a wall in the Cathedral housing project in Boston, boarded up, beaten, the worst of the worst, next to "Freddie as Mr. Kool," I found painted these words which lifted me and helped me write:

Dig inside yourself
See what you find

It could be something
You buried and kept buried
For a long time

Brothers and Sisters
Bring your buried treasure
To the surface of life.

notes

References to quotations and to some actual program examples are given below by page number. Notes here are selective, because of space, and because a complete listing of specific examples exceeds present knowledge. We don't yet have a directory of real-life community ideas arranged by topic and location.

Many other examples in the text were freely adapted from general sources cited in the section following. Still other examples were fictional for me, though possibly they are quite real for you.

Page 2 — Home and Garden Editor: *The Boston Globe* does this.

Page 3 — Karl Hess quote from his *Community Technology* (New York: Harper & Row, 1979), p. 36.

Page 3 — For starting skills banks, see Pat Saccomandi, *The Volunteer Skillsbank: An Innovative Way to Connect Individual Talents to Community Needs* (Boulder, Colo.: Volunteer: The National Training Center for Citizen Involvement, 1980, P. O. Box 4179, Boulder, CO 80306.) Skills exchanges often go beyond skill listing and usually involve more obligation; see, for example, R. Kay Fletcher and Stephen B. Fawcett, *The Skills Exchange* (Lawrence, Kan.: Institute of Public Affairs and Community Development, Division of Continuing Education, University of Kansas, no date).

Page 3 — Click and Clack are heard weekly on WBUR-FM, Boston.

Page 5 — Professors: Cf. the Boston Neighborhood Network, coordinated by Prof. Robert Hollister, Department of Urban and Environmental Policy, Tufts University, Medford, MA 02155.

Page 21 — Grey Bears: Contact California Grey Bears, 1298 Fair Avenue, Santa Cruz, CA 95060.

Page 25 — The bakers' lines are from Maurice Sendak, *In the Night Kitchen* (New York: Harper & Row, 1970). Punctuation modified.

Page 29 — Ad quote from *Barter and Trade Journal*, May, 1982, p.17. Journal is no longer published, but for further information contact Laura McCarthy, 925 Liberty Avenue, Rockland, MA 02370.

Page 31 — The Interest File: For one version, contact Susan McLucas, The Interest File, 18 Laurel Street, Cambridge, MA 02139.

Page 34 — Wally's Bus runs in Santa Monica, California. The vignette here, like many others in the text, is freely adapted.

Page 39 — Quote from Dylan Thomas, *Under Milk Wood* (New York: New Directions, 1954), p. 84.

Page 41 — Specific dress customs as observed in Ashland and Roseburg, Oregon.

Page 44 — Service quote from Michael Phillips and Sally Rasberry, *Honest Business: A Superior Strategy for Starting and Managing Your Own Business* (San Francisco: Clear Glass Publishing Co., and New York: Random House, 1981), p. 37.

Page 48 — QUBE was first introduced in Columbus, Ohio, in 1977. Further information is available from Warner Amex Cable Communications, Inc., 75 Rockefeller Plaza, New York, NY 10019.

Page 51 — Some cities publishing such catalogs: Lake Forest, Ill.; Lincoln, Neb.; Mt. Holly, N.J.; Detroit, Mich.

Page 55 — The Kansas Community Resource Act was passed in 1979 and is administered by the Kansas Department of Economic Development, 503 Kansas Avenue, Topeka, KS 66603.

Page 60 — Ethanol instructions from U.S. Office of Consumer Affairs, Consumer Information Division, *People Power: What Communities Are Doing to Counter Inflation* (Washington, D.C.: Author, 1980), pp. 213-215.

Pages 61 & 67 — Bonus bucks, Solar T-bills and Urban Ore: Related programs operate in Dallas and San Francisco. See *The Neighborhood Works* 4, no. 20 (November 16, 1981): pp. 12-13, p. 6.

Page 73 — Group house clearinghouse: Cf. New Community Projects, 449 Cambridge Street, Allston, MA 02134.

Pages 74-75 — Boarders: Data from historical research by Tamara Hareven, cited in *The Boston Globe*, April 11, 1980, p. 35.

Page 77 — Search and salvage: Cf. Tom Richard, *Rebound: A Guide to Community-Based Building Materials Recycling* (Seattle: Inner City Self Help Program, Central Area Motivation Program, 1982, 722 18th Avenue, Seattle, WA 98122).

Page 82 — Woods and shopping: Cf. the Swedish suburb of Farsta, outside of central Stockholm.

Page 85 — Menninger quote from *The New York Times*, November 13, 1975, p. 39.

Page 88 — Self-care quote from Bruce Stokes, "Self-Care: Best Kind of Health Insurance," *The Boston Globe*, August 10, 1979, p. 13.

Page 88 — *Healthy Choices* (1980) is available from Health Education Unit, LB-12C, Airdustrial Park, Building 2, Olympia WA 98504.

Page 89 — Seifert quote from *People Power*, op. cit., p. 356.

Page 99 — Nuclear poster: The hanging of such signs has been authorized for most nonresidential buildings in Boston by Boston's Board of Health and Hospitals. The poster is reprinted here by permission of the Department of Health and Hospitals, City of Boston, Massachusetts.

Page 103 — Spanish Fire Card: We produced such a card at our mental health center in Lowell, Mass.

Page 105 — Based on the Lyndon State College Rescue Squad, Lyndonville, Vermont.

Page 113 — Fuel efficiency: The daily wastes of 4000 people can produce 25 gallons of gasoline (plus fertilizer), which at 20 mpg yields 500 transit miles, with savings increasing excrementally if mass conveyances are used. Cf. the description of Littleton, Colo., in David Morris and Karl Hess, *Neighborhood Power: The New Localism* (Boston: Beacon Press, 1975), p. 130.

Page 116 — Among companies operating Samaritan Vans in the New England area are Consumer Value Stores (CVS), based in Woonsocket, R.I. CVS has emphasized hiring of ex-convicts to drive the vans.

Page 117 — "Truckers Get GED Diplomas": See story in *The Rural Community Education Report*, no. 16 (Spring, 1982): 1. (Published by University for Man, 1221 Thurston, Manhattan, KS 66502.)

Page 117 — Horse and Wagon quote from *The Neighborhood Works* 4, no. 21-22 (December 18, 1981, special issue): 5.

Page 119 — Carol Bly quote from her *Letters from the Country* (New York: Harper & Row, 1981), p. 123. Cf. especially the short essay which contains this quote, "Where Have All the Fifty-Five-Year-Olds Gone?"

Page 124 — Thomas Merton quote from his *Contemplation in a World of Action* (Garden City, N. Y.: Doubleday, 1971), p. 164.

Pages 126-127 — One model for this type of program is Transitional Employment Enterprises, Inc., 184 High Street, Boston, MA 02110.

Page 127 — Quote from Thomas More, *Utopia* (New York: Appleton-Century-Crofts, 1949), p. 38.

Page 136 — For money-making agency options, see William A. Duncan, *Looking at Income-Generating Businesses for Small Nonprofit Organizations* (Washington, D.C.: Center for Community Change, 1982, 1000 Wisconsin Avenue, N.W., Washington, D.C. 20007.) In Colorado Springs, the Pike's Peak Mental Health Center acquired a motel...(p. 19).

Page 141 — Max's story, "I Am (Emotionally) What I Eat," is found in *Men Sharing*, no. 2 (May, 1982): 5. (Published c/o Emerge, 25 Huntington Ave., Room 324, Boston, MA 02116.)

Pages 142-145 — Self-help clearinghouses exist in several states. One of the most well developed at this writing is the New Jersey Self-Help Clearinghouse, St. Clare's Hospital CMHC, Denville, NJ 07834.

Page 148 — The account of the Gilroy Garlic Festival comes from U.S. Department of Housing and Urban Development, Office of

Public Affairs, *The Urban Fair: How Cities Celebrate Themselves* (Washington, D. C.: Author, no date), pp. 35-36. Material here is directly quoted, but sentences are rearranged.

Page 148 — The sociologist is Amitai Etzioni, quoted in *The New York Times* (Sunday Travel Section), June 2, 1974, p. 25.

Page 161 — "Report a Pusher" quote from *The New York Times* (The Week in Review), November 14, 1982, p. 18E.

Page 163 — For a different perspective on information, see Manfred Kochen and Joseph C. Donohue, eds., *Information for the Community* (Chicago: American Library Association, 1976).

Page 165 — Form is reprinted from Saccomandi, op. cit., p. 7, by kind permission. In this instance, skills and interests are listed on the same page.

Page 170 — Thumbtack Bugle example comes from Phillips and Rasberry, op. cit., as do several other ideas adapted in the text.

Page 193 — Residents' Committee quote from Ruth Sidel, *Families of Fengsheng: Urban Life in China* (Baltimore: Penguin Books, 1974), p. 66.

Page 197 — On the costs of schizophrenia, see John G. Gunderson and Loren R. Mosher, "The Cost of Schizophrenia," *American Journal of Psychiatry* 132 (1975): 901-906. Figures are in 1975 dollars. The authors claim that the annual cost is equivalent to two percent of the gross national product (p. 903).

Page 198 — Navy jingle: Words are close, but may not be exact; memory fades.

Page 199 — Educare quote from Seymour B. Sarason, *Work, Aging, and Social Change: Professionals and the One Life - One Career Imperative* (New York: Free Press, 1975), p. 269. The comment on career decisions and mortality also derives from Sarason's work.

Page 206 — Harman plant experience is reported in Bruce Stokes, *Helping Ourselves: Local Solutions to Global Problems* (New York: W. W. Norton, 1981), p. 25 ff.

Page 209 — Edward Bellamy quote from his *Looking Backward* (New York: New American Library, 1960), p. 60.

Page 212 — Mrs. Kostritsky is quoted in Jane Jacobs, *The Death and Life of Great American Cities* (New York: Vintage, 1961), pp. 63-64.

Page 217 — Cinderella shoes: This and other unusual examples of public urban art are pictured in Ronald L. Fleming and Renata von Tscharner, with George Melrod, *Place Makers: Public Art That Tells You Where You Are* (Cambridge, Mass.: The Townscape Institute, Inc., and New York: Hastings House Publishers, 1981).

Page 223 — Adopt a rock: This program in New York's Central Park is described in Karin Carlson, *New York Self Help Handbook: A Step by Step Guide to Neighborhood Improvement Projects* (New York: The Citizens Committee for New York City, Inc., 1977, p. 63, 3 West 29th Street, New York, NY 10001).

Page 226 — Information on Pierre the Pelican is available from The National Mental Health Association, 1800 North Kent Street, Arlington, VA 22209.

Page 233 — The Christmas invitation vignette is based on a real event organized annually by Frank Bowes in Arlington, Mass.

...and note also: The community dreams in this book do not encompass all of community life. A section on schools is missing: so are sections on crime, courts, children, the elderly, and cooperatives, to name just a few. These are perhaps topics for a sequel.

sources

Sources for many of the ideas in this book are listed below. These are general sources, dream catalogs, not usually limited to one content area, and not usually detailing "how-to"; rather, they triggered my imagination, as I hope they may trigger yours.

The organizations mentioned here and in the "Notes" section preceding may also be contacted for further information.

Books

Allen, Patricia R. *Youthbook: Models and Resources for Neighborhood Use*. New York: The Citizens Committee for New York City, Inc., 1980. 3 West 29th Street, New York, NY 10001.

Brand, Stewart, ed. *The Next Whole Earth Catalog*. 2nd ed. New York: Random House, 1981.

Cala, Michael, with Susan Lob and Marian Sroge. *The Older Person's Handbook*. New York: Mutual Aid Project, 1979. 17 Murray Street, New York, NY 10007.

California State Office of Appropriate Technology, Community Assistance Group. *Working Together: Self-Reliance in California's Communities*. Sacramento, Calif.: Author, 1981. 1600 9th Street, Sacramento, CA 95814.

Callenbach, Ernest. *Ecotopia*. New York: Bantam Books, 1977.

Carlson, Karin. *New York Self Help Handbook: A Step by Step Guide to Neighborhood Improvement Projects*. New York: The Citizens Committee for New York City, Inc., 1977. 3 West 29th Street, New York, NY 10001.

Cassidy, Robert. *Livable Cities: A Grass-Roots Guide to Rebuilding Urban America*. New York: Holt, Rinehart and Winston, 1980.

Citizens Planning and Housing Association. *CPHA's Baltimore Neighborhood Self Help Handbook*. Baltimore: Author, 1982. 340 North Charles Street, Baltimore, MD 21201.

City of Dallas, Department of Urban Planning. *Neighborhood Notebook*. Dallas: Author, no date. Department of Planning and Development, 1500 Marilla Street, Suite 5-DN, Dallas, TX 75201.

Corbett, Michael N. *A Better Place to Live: New Designs for Tomorrow's Communities*. Emmaus, PA: Rodale Press, 1981.

Freundlich, Paul; Collins, Chris; and Wenig, Mikki. *A Guide to Cooperative Alternatives*. New Haven, CT and Louisa, VA: Community Publications Cooperative, 1979.

Hawken, Paul; Ogilvy, James; and Schwartz, Peter. *Seven Tomorrows: Toward a Voluntary History*. New York: Bantam Books, 1982.

Hess, Karl. *Community Technology*. New York: Harper & Row, 1979.

Jacobs, Jane. *The Death and Life of Great American Cities*. New York: Vintage, 1961.

Morris, David. *Self-Reliant Cities: Energy and the Transformation of Urban America*. San Francisco: Sierra Club Books, 1982.

Morris, David, and Hess, Karl. *Neighborhood Power: The New Localism*. Boston: Beacon Press, 1975.

National Commission on Neighborhoods. *People, Building Neighborhoods: Final Report to the President and the Congress of the United States*. Washington, D.C.: U.S. Government Printing Office, 1979.

New World Foundation. *Initiatives for Community Self-Help: Efforts to Increase Recognition and Support*. New York: Author, 1980. 100 East 85th Street, New York, NY 10028.

Phillips, Michael, and Rasberry, Salli. *Honest Business: A Superior Strategy for Starting and Managing Your Own Business*. San Francisco: Clear Glass Publishing Co., and New York: Random House, 1981.

Sale, Kirkpatrick. *Human Scale*. New York: Coward, McCann & Geoghegan, 1980.

Sidel, Ruth. *Families of Fengsheng: Urban Life in China.* Baltimore: Penguin Books, 1974.

Simple Living Collective (American Friends Service Committee, San Francisco). *Taking Charge: Achieving Personal and Political Change through Simple Living.* New York: Bantam Books, 1977.

Skinner, B.F. *Walden Two.* New York: Macmillan, 1948.

Stokes, Bruce. *Helping Ourselves: Local Solutions to Global Problems.* New York: W. W. Norton, 1981.

Trecker, Audrey R. and Harleigh B. *Handbook of Community Service Projects.* New York: Association Press, 1960.

U.S. Department of Housing and Urban Development, Office of Neighborhoods, Voluntary Associations, and Consumer Protection. *Neighborhoods: A Self-Help Sampler.* Washington, D.C.: Author, 1980.

U.S. Office of Consumer Affairs, Consumer Information Division. *People Power: What Communities Are Doing to Counter Inflation.* Washington, D.C.: Author, 1980.

Washington Consulting Group, Inc. *Uplift: What People Themselves Can Do.* Salt Lake City: Olympus Publishing Co., 1974.

Journals and Newsletters

Citizen Participation (Lincoln Filene Center, Tufts University, Medford, MA 02155).

CoEvolution Quarterly (P.O. Box 428, Sausalito, CA 94966).

Communities: Journal of Cooperation (P.O. Box 426, Louisa, VA 23093).

Conserve Neighborhoods (National Trust for Historic Preservation, 1785 Massachusetts Avenue, N.W., Washington, D.C. 20036).

The Futurist (World Future Society, 4916 St. Elmo Avenue, Bethesda, MD 20814).

Leading Edge Bulletin (P.O. Box 42247, Los Angeles, CA 90042).

Local Initiatives (Applied Information Resources, Inc., 700-B Garfield Building, 19 Garfield Place, Cincinnati, OH 45202).

McCall's (See especially "Survival in the Suburbs" column, in back issues only, as well as similar sections in related "women's magazines.")

The Neighborhood Works (Center for Neighborhood Technology, 570 West Randolph Street, Chicago, IL 60606).

New Options (P. O. Box 19324, Washington, D.C. 20036).

Public Management (International City Management Association, 1120 G Street, N.W., Washington, D.C. 20005).

RAIN: Journal of Appropriate Technology (2270 NW Irving, Portland, OR 97210).

ruralamerica (Rural America, 1900 M Street, N.W., Washington, D.C. 20036).

Self-Help Reporter (National Self-Help Clearinghouse, 33 West 42nd Street, Room 1222, New York, NY 10036).

Sharing (Project SHARE, P.O. Box 2309, Rockville, MD 20852).

Ways and Means (Conference on Alternative State and Local Policies, 2000 Florida Avenue, N.W., Washington, D.C. 20009).

The following newsletters are no longer being published, but back issues are worth consulting:

Dialogues (SNAP Support System, 124 West Kearsley Street, Suite 5000, Flint, MI 48502).

Self-Reliance (Institute for Local Self-Reliance, 1717 18th Street, N.W., Washington, D.C. 20009).

Would there also be use for a *Journal of New Community Ideas*?

Miscellaneous

Partnerships Dataline U.S.A. maintains a computerized data bank with thousands of case examples of community problem-solving efforts nationwide. Information and selected printouts may be obtained by calling (800) 223-6004, or by contacting its parent organization, Citizens Forum on Self-Government/National Municipal League, at 55 West 44th Street, New York, NY 10036.

an invitation

You have read about my dreams: I would like to read about yours.

Across America, I believe there are thousands of community ideas like those mentioned here, but different and often better. Yet many of them are secreted, forgotten, half buried and left for dead. They don't get publicized because their creators are not writers and because they wouldn't know how or where to publicize them outside of their own communities. There's also no incentive for doing so. How can we provide one?

I envision a sequel to this book, richer and more exciting than this one, of community dreams and real community actions of your own. I see a network of dreamers from coast to coast. I'd like to find a place for regular publication of new community ideas as they are thought up and implemented. We can start right here.

So I ask you to send me your dreams and your realities, in a paragraph or two or more, in whatever form makes most sense for you. What new ideas have worked in your community? What could work if given a chance? Be fanciful, or specific; let your mind run free.

All replies will be acknowledged. If there are enough, I will try to arrange for their publication, with proper credit to contributors. If you take a step, a bank of dreams may be closer than we think.

Address your response to:

Community Dreams
Impact Publishers
Post Office Box 1094
San Luis Obispo, California 93406

Thank you.

acknowledgements

The cover and chapter introduction art for this book were drawn by Diane and Joel Schatz of Transition Graphics, Salem, Oregon. The work is based upon their copyrighted "Ecotopia" and "Community Alert" series of posters, produced in conjunction with RAIN magazine, the National Council of Churches, and the U. S. Department of Energy.

Judy Bellizia typed the manuscript to its fruition; once again she made an editor's life easier.

My wife, Madelon, supported the manuscript from its inception; once again, she made a writer's life possible.

Impact Publishers' books are available at booksellers throughout the U.S.A. and in many other countries. If you are not able to find a title of interest at a nearby bookstore, we would be happy to fill your direct order. Please send us:

1. Complete name, address and zip code information
2. The full title of the book(s) you want
3. The number of copies of each book
4. California residents add 6% sales tax
5. $1.00 shipping for the first book; $.25 for each additional book.

VISA and MasterCard are acceptable; be sure to include complete card number, expiration date and your authorizing signature. Send your order to **Impact Publishers, Post Office Box 1094, San Luis Obispo, CA 93406**, or call us at **805-543-5911**.